# WATER EFFECTS
# IN THE GARDEN

Gilly Love

# WATER EFFECTS
## simple ways to achieve beautiful water features
# IN THE GARDEN

consultant Peter Robinson
photographer Sarah Cuttle

aquamarine

This edition is published by Aquamarine

Aquamarine is an imprint of Anness Publishing Ltd
Hermes House, 88–89 Blackfriars Road,
London SE1 8HA
tel. 020 7401 2077; fax 020 7633 9499
www.aquamarinebooks.com; info@anness.com

© Anness Publishing Ltd 2001, 2005

UK agent: The Manning Partnership Ltd,
6 The Old Dairy, Melcombe Road, Bath BA2 3LR;
tel. 01225 478444; fax 01225 478440;
sales@manning-partnership.co.uk

UK distributor: Grantham Book Services Ltd,
Isaac Newton Way, Alma Park Industrial Estate,
Grantham, Lincs NG31 9SD; tel. 01476 541080;
fax 01476 541061; orders@gbs.tbs-ltd.co.uk

North American agent/distributor: National Book
Network, 4501 Forbes Boulevard, Suite 200,
Lanham, MD 20706; tel. 301 459 3366;
fax 301 429 5746; www.nbnbooks.com

Australian agent/distributor
Pan Macmillan Australia, Level 18, St Martins Tower,
31 Market St, Sydney, NSW 2000; tel. 1300 135
113; fax 1300 135 103;
customer.service@macmillan.com.au

New Zealand agent/distributor: David Bateman Ltd,
30 Tarndale Grove, Off Bush Road, Albany,
Auckland; tel. (09) 415 7664; fax (09) 415 8892

A CIP catalogue record for this book is available
from the British Library.

Publisher  Joanna Lorenz
Editorial Director  Judith Simons
Executive Editor  Caroline Davison
Designer  Ruth Hope
Photographer  Sarah Cuttle
Stylist  Gilly Love
Editorial Reader  Richard McGinlay
Production Controller  Claire Rae

Previously published as *Water in the Garden*
1 2 3 4 5 6 7 8 9 10

**Note to reader** Some of the projects require
an electric power supply to circulate the water.
It is important to ask a qualified electrician to
install any outside power supply. The publisher
cannot be held responsible for any accident or
injury that may occur as a result of using this book.

# contents

Water is one of the most important ingredients of life. In so many cultures, both ancient and contemporary, it symbolizes the vital energy without which there would be no life on earth. It is the element that is most deeply connected to all the human senses. We all have an intense and primal affinity with water – think of the sensual pleasure experienced from the sound of waves breaking on a beach or the thunderous rush as pebbles are dragged by a powerful undertow. Consider the sight of sun sparkling on a rippling stream; the smell of wet grass after summer rain; the comfort and relaxing effect of a long, hot bath; the stimulation of a powerful and refreshing shower; and, finally, the clean taste and incomparable thirst-quenching impact of cool, clear, fresh water.

**right** The addition of water brings a new dimension to the garden as it falls from one level to another – in these cases in a series of lipped bowls, down a narrow rill or over smooth stones. The sound of gentle cascading has a calming effect on the senses.

introduction

Since the earliest civilizations the garden has been symbolic of a paradise on earth, the creation of a personal piece of heaven. Even the word "paradise" comes from *paradeisos*, the Greek for garden.

Gardens have taken many forms, but water has always been an essential element. Previous generations created complicated devices in order to ensure a constant water pressure in fountains where they could not rely on the force of a natural spring; artificial ponds and lakes required painstaking digging by hand, followed by the introduction of vast amounts of clay to achieve a watertight base. Today's gardeners, by contrast, have the technology to control and manipulate the flow of water, often merely at the flick of a switch; in addition, excavating machinery makes the installation of ponds and lakes fast and simple.

What does remain eminently valid from past generations, however, is the wealth of ingenious ideas and magical interpretations that offer endless inspiration for creating truly individual water features for our gardens, from natural ponds that attract wildlife to sophisticated, computer-operated jets that produce ever-changing water patterns.

**right** The rill, a narrow channel of water, was used extensively in Islamic gardens to link one pool to another. This modern rill leads the eye to a deep pool and a gushing spout dramatically lit from below.

**far right** Sculpting with water has fascinated generations of garden designers. The striking contemporary sculpture in the centre of the garden is an acrylic sphere. The water is pumped over the surface to create an illusory effect. The sphere creates constant movement and ever-changing reflections.

# the appeal of water

Water wears many different guises in nature, and each has its own

distinctive beauty – from dewdrops shining in the morning sun, to

the intricate patterns formed by frost and the crisp sparkle of snow.

**above** We often overlook the simple things in life, but even dew or raindrops shimmering on a leaf can hold exquisite beauty if we take the time to look closely.

Since water is such a vital component of life in all its forms, it is perhaps not surprising that people have always had a deep, instinctive response to it. Quite apart from its physical necessity in sustaining life, drawing people to live near to water sources for practical reasons, we seem to derive a profound sense of satisfaction from its presence. Still water, in the form of lakes or quiet pools, can induce a deep tranquillity as we contemplate its mirror-like surface or gaze into the depths and glimpse the shadowy world of fish and other creatures. Rivers and streams, with their constant movement, present a different picture, but one that is equally conducive to peaceful

**right** Waterlilies floating on the surface of a deep, calm pool, swaying gently with the movement of the water, offer balm to the spirits with their ethereal beauty.

**left** Nothing else in nature can match the extraordinary transformation brought about by a fall of snow. Overnight, the world becomes an enchanted, magical place.

contemplation, with the gentle sound and ever-changing patterns of light producing an almost hypnotic effect. Water is also symbolic of purity and cleansing, and moving water can have a purifying, uplifting effect on our spirits.

Not many of us are fortunate enough to possess a natural lake or a stream running through our gardens, but such is the appeal of water that people have always gone to great lengths to introduce them artificially, scaled down to an appropriate level. For some, it may be the sound of moving water that is most important, and this can be created by fountains of all kinds, even if you only have room for a small container. If it is the wildlife that you are more interested in, a natural-looking pond can be created, to offer habitats to a wide variety of creatures. This can be of great benefit to the overall balance of life in the garden and reduce many of the problems caused by pests – for example, frogs and toads will eat large quantities of slugs, and the birds will help to control many insect pests. There is also the reward of feeling that we have contributed in a small way to the natural environment, and the microcosm of life that is created in a wildlife pond can be a fascinating study in itself.

Whatever our reasons for introducing water into the garden, whether an elaborate feature or a simple small pool, it is guaranteed to add an extra dimension, and to help make the garden into a place of beauty, harmony and healing.

**right** The garden may not seem so inviting on cold winter days, but the delicate tracery of frost can be as lovely in its way as the more obvious attractions of summer.

# cultural influences

Water has been used in the garden by many cultures. Islamic water

gardens, the Moorish gardens of Spain, as well as Renaissance and

Zen gardens have all influenced the design of water gardens today.

In the ancient world, water fulfilled both practical and symbolic roles. The Egyptians conserved the annual flood waters of the Nile in vast reservoirs from which irrigation systems watered crops for the rest of the year, and in their gardens they created still pools and canals not only for quiet contemplation but also to stock with fish and water birds for the provision of constant fresh food.

Water was also essential in the gardens of ancient Persia, which were created for relaxation, and to symbolize the presence of life in sharp contrast to the surrounding mountainous and desert landscape. Centrally placed reservoirs were eminently practical for cooling the atmosphere and providing the means for cultivation but were also symbolic of wealth and prosperity.

**left** The smooth, glass-like surface of this still, formal pool is highly reflective, perfect for quiet contemplation and gentle relaxation.

## Islamic water gardens

The vital importance of gardens to Persian culture had been evolving for more than a thousand years when, in AD 637, the empire was overrun by the Islamic Arabs. Traditionally these nomads moved constantly, trekking from one oasis to another in the search for water. The spiritual fused with the practical in the continuing development of the Islamic garden for nearly a thousand years, and its influence spread as far as Moorish Spain in the west and Mogul India to the east. The gardens, often square but sometimes rectangular, were divided into four because, according to Islamic beliefs, the universe was divided by four rivers into four squares, with one central spring representing life.

According to the Koran, paradise is a garden flowing with water, wine, milk and honey – represented by the four rivers. This quartered pattern was often repeated in larger gardens as it was essential to be always within the sight and sound of water. The outer square or rectangle represented order and nature, while a central circle was symbolic of heaven. The interplay between the square and the circle had a great influence on Islamic architecture as well as garden design, and the classic fourfold garden created a cool and protected sanctuary from the scorching desert beyond its walls.

**left** The formal outline of this long canal-like pool is echoed by the symmetry of the planting.

**above** One of the most beautiful water features in the world is the famous canal and two rows of single water jets at the Generalife in Granada, Spain.

## The Moorish influence in Spain

At the beginning of the 8th century, the Moors invaded southern Spain from north-west Africa, and remained there until the 15th century when Boabdil, the last Moorish king, finally surrendered Granada to the Christian King Fernando and Queen Isabel. The subtropical climate and mountainous terrain of Andalucia were such that water was at a premium, and the Moors reintroduced the hydraulic and irrigation systems that had been long forgotten since the departure of the Romans centuries before.

One of the most famous examples of Moorish design is the Generalife at Granada, built on the hillside of the Cerro del Sol, as a palace for the ruling kings. The name is taken from the original Arabic, meaning "the garden of the architect", and the entire design is the relation between successive areas of garden. In the Patio de la Riadh a long, narrow canal runs the entire length of the garden. Arcaded loggias provide cool shade, and at either end of the canal are lotus-shaped basins whose low bubble fountains cause the water to continually brim over. A later addition was the two rows of single jets that arch across the canal to create a visual delight and a cooling mist in the searing heat of high summer. Water cascades down the carved channels of the balustrades of the water stairway and tiny fountains sparkle and tinkle into circular pools at the bottom of each flight of steps. The Alhambra Palace, situated below the Generalife, was designed as a fortress but also includes four garden courtyards, each following the Islamic quadripartite design with a central pool and channels leading from it. Each of these courtyards is very different but the entrance to each one is preceded by a series of enclosed passages. These symbolize leaving the dark to enter the heavenly sunlight and the garden of paradise.

## The Islamic influence in India

The influence of Islamic gardens spread into India with the Moguls, and the gardens of the Taj Mahal in Agra are a supreme example. The emperor Shah Jahan built this mausoleum between 1632 and 1654 for his wife Mumtaz Mahal, a Persian princess, and the gardens around it represented the paradise to which her departed spirit would go. The gardens follow the fourfold design divided by marble-lined canals, and when it was first built, these canals were bordered with avenues of cypress (symbolizing death and eternity) and fruit trees (for life and fertility), and with sunken beds filled with pale, scented flowers. Both the Persians and the Moguls loved to spend time in their gardens in the cool of the evening, and the pale flowers, such as lilies, roses and jasmine, would glow in the light of the moon, filling the air with their perfume. In order to provide water for these plants, and for the canals and fountains, the Mogul architects created a system where water was fed through underground pipes by a series of purs – a means by which water is drawn from the river using ropes and buckets pulled by bullocks to a vast storage tank. Water was transferred via overhead channels and raised tanks to a level that ensured a constant water pressure in the fountains.

## Europe and the Renaissance

A very different world view from that of Islam was expressed in the Renaissance movement, which had meanwhile been sweeping across Europe, originating in Italy around the 15th century. Inspired by classical Greek and Roman architecture, and with a philosophy based on humanity's superiority and domination over the natural world, the Renaissance style was ordered, formal and often highly elaborate.

**right** The formality and symmetry of this large-scale pool are created by the neat regularity of the classical bridge, with its series of arches that are beautifully reflected on the surface of the water.

The two cities at the forefront of Renaissance garden design were Rome and Florence and since their surrounding landscape was hilly, it became a feature to create gardens in a series of terraces where water would run down through a series of channels and cascades with an impressive feature at the top of the garden and another spectacle at the bottom near the villa. The order and formality of the design was a legacy from the Romans, but whereas Roman gardens had been enclosed by high protective walls, the new style was more open, reflecting the greater political stability in Europe. The Christian Church also supported the idea of controlling nature, believing that this was an imitation of God's power on earth.

Many of Italy's ingenious waterworks were designed by the Francinis, a talented family of craftsmen. In the late 16th century, they went to France to work for King Henri IV, thus helping to promote the Italian style there. The French embraced the idea of formal water features on a grand scale, and in 1661 the great landscape designer André Le Nôtre completed his first project, Vaux-le-Vicomte. The moated château was a well-established tradition in France, but as well as a moat Le Nôtre introduced a large sunken canal in front of the château, adding an element of surprise as it is not visible at first glance. The French king Louis XIV was so impressed with the heroic grandeur of this creation that he took it over for himself, forcibly removing the owner, and commissioned Le Nôtre to design the still more magnificent gardens at his famous palace of Versailles.

## The Zen garden

In ancient China, gardens were designed to reflect nature rather than to change it, with a careful balance maintained between yin and yang, the two opposing forces pervading the universe. Yin, the feminine, dark, negative, passive and cold aspect of nature, was represented in the landscape by water, and yang, the masculine, light, positive, active and hot aspect, by rocks, hills or mountains. The Zen Buddhism of Japan developed these ideas, and gardens became a central part of the religion, always with the emphasis on harmony and meditation. Water features were created in naturalistic shapes, and moving water was believed to promote the flow of ch'i (life force). In some Zen gardens, no actual water is present, but it is represented symbolically by gravel raked into patterns to imitate ripples or waves.

**left** Bridges or stepping stones are an important feature of the Zen garden. They provide a perfect place in which to meditate, providing closer proximity to the water. The effect is enhanced by the gentle splashing of water from a bamboo spout.

**right** Water is a vital feature in the Zen garden as it represents the yin force. It is often imitated by sand or gravel, which is meticulously raked to emulate ripples or waves breaking against significant and large stones. The raking of the ground is a meditative practice in itself.

The concept of conserving water is as ancient as civilization itself. Water has always been, and remains, a very precious commodity that is vital to life.

Over the centuries, different cultures have created widely varying methods of keeping water in one place. Some reservoirs were for the soul, such as the spiritual pools found in Japanese gardens, others were extremely practical, such as the impluvium, or marble-lined gutters, devised by the Romans to collect rain water used for irrigation, while yet others were purely decorative, like the vast formal stretches in the French classical gardens. Whether it be a simple stone basin, a naturalistic pond or a contemporary swimming pool, there are numerous ways of containing water that will enhance the design of the garden and suit its topography.

**right** Reservoirs may be pools and ponds reflecting the surrounding trees and plants or may be gardens in their own right, filled with the lush flowers and foliage of aquatic and marginal plants. Alternatively, they can be as simple as a series of shallow, water-filled bowls.

reservoir

Before making a decision regarding the style and form of your water feature, it is important to take into account the surrounding features and buildings. The ambient climate, the topography and the aspect of the site will also have an impact, particularly in terms of budget for both initial installation and, in some cases, maintenance. Creating a harmonious fusion between house and garden, budget and aspiration requires judicious and considered planning. It is important from the outset to be very clear about what you want to achieve.

Formal ponds may be positioned to reflect statuary or sculpture, architectural plants or elegant trees. As a contrast, keen horticulturists may be attracted to a more informal-looking pond, which both encourages wildlife into the garden and offers endless planting possibilities, particularly if it incorporates an area of bog garden.

**above** A circle of water has been used in this garden design to express a void through which life, represented by aquatic mint, emerges. The circle is surrounded by decking to indicate the human presence.

**right** In this garden, modern materials such as steel and Perspex (Plexiglass) are exploited to contain moving water within a gleaming tiered arrangement. The formal pools are echoed by a checked pattern of blue glass "gravel" and undulating moss.

# pools and ponds

Even the smallest expanse of still water is a natural mirror – capturing all the beauty of the surrounding plants and trees and the sky above in its ever-changing reflections.

**above** A lake design, typical of the English Landscape Movement, featuring a false bridge with its arches repeated in the curved niches of the hedge above.

Ponds and pools can be as large or small as you like, but for easier maintenance and to create a harmonious balance of plants and aquatic life, the bigger the better; certainly anything less than 2.4m (8ft) square will be difficult to sustain. Depth is also important: a minimum of 45–60cm (18–24in) is sufficient for the smallest pond, and this will avoid the growth of green algae, which thrives in warm shallow water. Your preferred choice of plants will also determine the optimum position and size, just as for any other form of garden feature. As a general rule, avoid full shade, whether created by buildings or walls or, worse still, overhanging trees, whose falling leaves are a menace to healthy waterlife.

A further point to consider is the proximity of the house to the proposed site in terms of electrical installations, such as pumps or lighting.

## Formal

Although formal ponds have a history that dates back to the Romans and Persians, they are ideal for the contemporary garden, terrace or patio. Their strong geometric shapes can be circles, rectangles, squares, ellipses or long narrow channels, always with clearly defined solid edges.

Any expanse of water situated close to a house is best considered as an extension of the existing architecture, and so its dimensions need to be in proportion to the building's height and width to be aesthetically pleasing. As part of a terrace or patio, the pond needs to sit comfortably within a hard landscaping pattern rather than cut across it, and

**below** Despite the formal and geometric lines of this contemporary pool, it captures the natural mystery of a meandering stream.

**above** Water and ancient olive trees convey a sense of peace and continuity in this enclosed garden. It features renowned sculptor William Pye's sensational "Vortex of Water".

paving may be constructed to overhang the water's surface to conceal the inner lining. To create the best reflections of adjacent buildings, the base of the pond must be dark, preferably black, and if it is positioned in a sunny site, light will be reflected back in the form of magical shafts into the walls and ceilings of interior rooms.

Perfectly constructed formal ponds may need little or no further embellishment, as it is the stillness and tranquillity that is the essence of their beauty. Any planting requires restraint and meticulous upkeep to maintain the formality. If reflection is not essential, then waterlilies, planted in containers to restrain them from taking over the pond, are a good choice because they are visually attractive both at ground level and from above.

**above** Sagittaria, also
known as the swamp
potato, is an excellent
marginal plant for
informal ponds and has
tiny white flowers during
the summer months.

## Informal

When the position of a pond is farther away from the house,
a more natural-looking shape may be preferable, unless the
style of the garden is very formal, in which case the pond's
contours need to follow the geometric lines of trees, shrubs
or lawn designs. While formal ponds are extrovert and
immediately obvious, an informal pond can embody
seclusion and secrecy. It might be a place that is
discovered partially concealed by tall plants such as
bamboo or an evergreen hedge, which would provide a
protected place in which to sit and enjoy the feature.

Ideally, an informal pond needs to be designed and
planned so carefully that it is impossible to tell that it was
artificially created. Such ponds can take the form of natural
pools, where the edge merges invisibly into the foliage and
flowers, as it would in the wild, with indigenous plants allowed to spread and
self-seed freely. By varying the depth of the water, you can broaden the scope
of the planting from marginals to aquatics, with moisture-loving plants around
the perimeter.

You may prefer to construct a natural-looking pond with a defined edge,
which is not only more easy to maintain than one that merges naturally with the
undergrowth but also allows you to get close to the water's edge. This margin
may actually be quite formal in shape, with paving, such as stones or bricks,
matching other materials used in the garden, and softened with low-level
planting or incorporating planting pockets for larger specimens.

**right** The presence of
a sheltering rustic woven
fence and a wood-
decked seating area
all contribute to the
countryside atmosphere
created around this
densely planted pond.
The pond, teeming
with fish and aquatic
creatures, is set in the
secluded part of an
urban garden.

**left** A naturalistic
waterfall nestling within
a rock garden contrasts
with the smooth
semicircular slate
paving and the
bright yellow-green
evergreen planting.

## Wildlife

Water naturally attracts all kinds of wildlife, from birds and small amphibians to insects and tiny aquatic creatures, and to create a healthy pond it is essential to establish the right balance of ingredients.

Oxygenating plants help to balance the delicate aquatic ecosystem and keep down the levels of green algae. The smaller the pond, the more prone it is to the growth of algae, which creates green, but otherwise harmless, water. Provided the water smells sweet, there is nothing to worry about. Some oxygenating plants are notoriously invasive, but the better-behaved species, such as *Eleocharis acicularis* and *Myriophyllum spicatum*, both have a feathery appearance underwater and provide shade and shelter for tadpoles, newts and pond snails. *Aponogeton distachyos* is an excellent oxygenator and one of the very few submerged aquatics that remains active during winter.

Waterlilies would seem an obvious choice, but if they are allowed to dominate a small pond their leaves block out the light and the oxygenators just refuse to grow. If, however, they are restrained in a container, their pads will provide a flat surface on which frogs and toads can sun themselves.

A collection of marginal plants around a wildlife pond creates a safe refuge for amphibians, and tall straight stems provide a place for emerging dragonfly larvae. A series of large stones or rocks will encourage newts, frogs and toads to take up residence, as they prefer to spend the winter on land in a frost-free location. It is an essential requirement of a wildlife pond that animals and birds can not only reach the water easily but can also get out again. For this to happen, you need to provide at least one gently shelving edge to act as a beach for wildlife. For larger ponds and lakes, you may consider acquiring some aquatic birds, but be warned that they may eat your choicest plants.

**left** Dense and luxurious planting, including primulas, astilbes, lobelias and the gigantic foliage of *Gunnera manicata*, envelops the streams and lagoons of this lush, tranquil water garden.

**right** An enchanting woodland setting where the trees planted close to the water's edge create exquisite reflections, provide dappled shade and emphasize the atmosphere of seclusion and privacy.

# *case study*  urban wildlife pond

A piece of outdoor personal space is vital for many urban dwellers, and this tiny

garden captures the charm of the countryside with the added pleasure of a

pocket-sized pond teeming with aquatic plants and animals.

This wildlife pond illustrates the possibility of creating an extraordinary garden that resembles a lush piece of countryside even though it is actually located in a city. In a seemingly impossibly small space, the garden includes a patch of wild flower meadow, established fruit trees, old-fashioned roses, at least eight varieties of ground-covering cranesbill and many types of indigenous thymes and lavender.

The wildlife pond at the far end of the garden enjoys the late afternoon sun and is the most sheltered and warm spot in which to sit on summer evenings. In view of the hazards of combining open water and young children, there is a small picket fence and secure gate to divide the lawn from the marsh garden and its adjoining pond. An old piece of carpet has been used to line the base of the shallow excavation, which is no more than 3m (10ft) square, and the edges of the butyl liner have been concealed with pieces of reclaimed slate and bricks. This hard edge on two sides gives easy access to the water and provides a place from which birds can drink. Children are inevitably fascinated by ponds, so even in a garden like this, where the water is only 50cm (20in) deep at its deepest point, you should never allow them to play there unless accompanied.

Only two years from its conception, the pond is already bursting with tiny aquatic animals introduced from a bucket of pond water. In spring, frogs and toads abound, although they are regularly culled by the local fox. Later in summer, bees and butterflies are attracted to the several species of *Iris brevicaulis*, *Ranunculus flammula*, *Lobelia cardinalis* and *Mentha aquatica* that have been planted around the pond's edge.

**below** By springtime, the pond is brimming with frog spawn, tadpoles and scores of other aquatic creatures. It is intriguing to watch them develop and mature.

**right** Lush planting on three sides of the pond conceals and blurs the edges. This completely convincing naturalistic effect has been created in less than two years since conception.

**above** The scented leaves of *Geranium* (cranesbill) are virtually evergreen and provide ground cover between the wild flower meadow and the outskirts of the pond.

**below** A discreet picket fence is both decorative and practical, providing a protective barrier to prevent a child from wandering down to the pond alone.

## *project* mosaic pond

This stunning pond is perfect for a small town garden, especially if it is sited near to a patio so that you can admire it while entertaining or dining *al fresco* on long summer evenings. You might even be tempted to dangle your feet in the cooling water after a long day at work. Children will enjoy splashing in the water as well, although for safety reasons, it is better to join in with them.

It is also relatively easy to create, being a simple, galvanized metal pond that is dug into the ground. This means that you do not have to fit a flexible liner or make the pond from concrete. The design can be varied according to personal taste, but an abstract pattern with a subdued colour scheme is both attractive and sophisticated. It is useful to sketch out your idea for the design on a piece of paper first before buying the tiles.

**above and right** The wooden decking surround is designed to overhang the side of the pond, which has a sharp edge. The pieces of tile are cut in a random fashion but stuck down to create meandering curves.

**above** Tile nippers are essential to ensure that there is a clean edge on each piece of tile and mirror.

**above** Smooth beach pebbles conceal the area where the decking meets the lawn. Evergreen plants, *Fatsia japonica* and *Pleioblastus pygmaeus*, and the strikingly coloured shrub *Ceratostigma willmottianum*, provide a lush background to the pond.

**above** Children are drawn to water whatever the weather, and need to be supervised until they are old enough to appreciate the dangers.

## You will need

| | |
|---|---|
| *Outdoor tiles in a selection of greens and blues* | *Nails* |
| | *Wooden decking* |
| *Hammer* | *Jigsaw* |
| *Sack cloth* | *Tile adhesive* |
| *Spade* | *Adhesive spreader* |
| *Galvanized metal pond, 1.2m (4ft) in diameter and 60cm (2ft) deep* | *Tile nippers* |
| | *Sheet of mirror* |
| | *Gloves* |
| *Sand* | *Goggles* |
| *Spirit (carpenter's) level* | *Glue and glue gun* |
| | *Grout* |
| | *Grout spreader* |
| *Piece of chalk* | *Sponge* |

**1** Mark out the design on a piece of paper. This does not have to be to scale, but will give you some idea of the pattern and the colour arrangement.

**2** Smash the tiles using a hammer and some sack cloth. Do each colour separately.

**3** Dig a hole in the ground to accommodate the pond. Bed the pond in with a layer of sand. You will probably have to try the pond in the hole a few times until you get a good fit. Check that it is level. Using a piece of chalk, mark out the design on the bottom of the pond.

**4** (*left*) Construct the decking by nailing the wooden planks to two cross supports to create a rectangular shape, and then cut out the oval shape with a jigsaw. Lay the oval-shaped piece of decking over the pond, and check that it is level using a spirit level.

**5** (*right*) Spread a layer of tile adhesive over the first part of the design using an adhesive spreader.

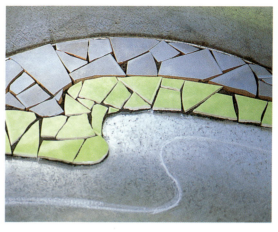

**6** Stick the broken pieces of tile along the edge, but within the chalk line. Fill in the inside area. Use tile nippers to get the perfect shape (*see inset, above*). Finish this colour band.

**7** Start on the next colour, sticking down the tiles around the edge inside the chalk line as before. Finish this colour.

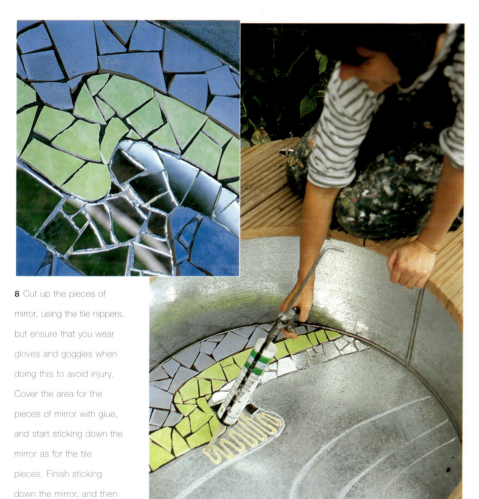

**8** Cut up the pieces of mirror, using the tile nippers, but ensure that you wear gloves and goggles when doing this to avoid injury. Cover the area for the pieces of mirror with glue, and start sticking down the mirror as for the tile pieces. Finish sticking down the mirror, and then stick down the last colour (*see inset, above*).

**9** Allow the mosaic work to dry for three days. Grout the bottom of the pond with the mosaic grout, using the grout spreader.

**10** Clean with a damp sponge.

# raised pools

Raised or semi-raised pools are not as nature intended, but for small gardens where there is no soft landscaping they offer numerous design possibilities that bring water closer to eye level.

Water contained within a solid structure that raises it above the ground requires no excavation, which is an important consideration in many town gardens where access is through the house. Such features are ideally constructed in conjunction with the design and installation of a terrace or patio and where the materials are chosen to co-ordinate with the surrounding architecture and flooring. While the basic construction is similar to formal ponds, it is worth considering making the coping wide enough for sitting on or for safely positioning large containers.

Elevating water does, of course, mean that it may be subjected to greater temperature fluctuations – it may overheat in summer and be prone to freezing in winter – but this problem may be overcome by siting the pool in a more shady position and designing it with greater depth. Set against a wall, this style of pool may also incorporate a circulating system that spills water from a mascaron, or wall mask, or simple spout, which both cools the atmosphere and adds the musical element of sound. With the addition of lighting, such water features create an idyllic spot in which to sit at twilight on a warm summer evening.

Raised pools are a safer option for small children using the garden, but care is still imperative, and a rustproof removable metal grid is a worthwhile safety consideration. Routine maintenance is much simpler with a raised pool, as it is less prone to garden debris such as dead leaves, and water can be easily siphoned out when the pool needs to be cleaned. Combined with a small fountain, a raised pool provides a perfect environment for fish, since the spray effectively oxygenates the water.

# wet gardens

Marsh or wet gardens may be self-contained features within a larger garden but, when linked to an expanse of water, they are best associated with informal ponds, either natural or artificially created.

**above** The perennial *Dierama pulcherrimum* combines the arching elegance of reed-like leaves with the colour of delicate rose-pink flowers in the summer.

**right** The planting schemes of wet gardens need as careful planning as any other garden border. Choose a good contrast of leaf colour, texture and shape.

**below** A large clump of dusty pink astilbes contrast in both colour and texture to the more sparsely planted purple blues of the *Iris ensata*.

**below right** The exquisite flowers of these irises appear in mid- to late spring and are a perfect companion for candelabra primulas.

Although marsh or wet gardens are often called bog gardens, in the wild a true bog is a very specialized type of wet ground that is usually completely self-contained and relies entirely on regular rainfall to maintain the delicate ecological balance. The highly acidic peaty environment is built up over thousands of years by the continual decomposition of floating vegetative material and sphagnum moss. Water replaces air in the soil and only certain plants will flourish in these anaerobic conditions.

Acid-loving plants such as butterworts, bladderworts and orchids are true bog plants, but will not thrive in an artifically watered marsh or wet garden. Most moisture-loving plants cannot tolerate the waterlogged conditions of a wet garden, where water has replaced the air in the soil, as they need more air than water to secure the nutrients vital to their growth. However, there are some marginal or shallow-water plants that can adapt to or at least tolerate drier conditions and may be considered moisture-loving too.

There is a wide range of non-invasive plants suitable for the wet garden, but, as with any planting scheme, only careful planning will achieve the right balance of colour, texture and seasonal interest. Try sweet flags, marsh marigolds, flowering rushes and the elegant water irises to create a spectacular display.

# canals and rills

Smooth, silent and peaceful water typifies the broad channel of a canal

whereas the smaller the rill the more water is confined to a narrow gorge

where it can be forced to rush and gush with considerable power.

Historically, the canal was the most significant water feature in the gardens of ancient Egypt, Rome and Islam, and these numerous inventive designs influenced the grand constructions in post-Renaissance Europe that can still be seen in the classical gardens of France, the Netherlands and Germany.

Few of the Dutch-inspired canals constructed in the grand English gardens of the 17th century survived the sweeping changes of the 18th-century Landscape Movement, which eschewed the formality of features such as canals and rills. However, in the early part of the 20th century, the renowned architect Edwin Lutyens (1869–1944) incorporated canals in his designs for gardens. He designed houses and gardens simultaneously, often in partnership with the great plantswoman Gertrude Jekyll (1843–1932), and his integration of rectangular canals and water tanks provided a gentle contrast to the complex architectural detailing and intense planting schemes. Lutyens created one of the most impressive 20th century neoclassical garden designs, at Tyringham in Buckinghamshire, England. Here a canal, some 270m (900ft) long, sweeps from the house to the garden's edge, and is only interrupted by a circular pool.

In contrast to the canal, the rill is traditionally a much narrower channel of water and is often used in garden design to give a natural impression by winding gently like the course of a natural stream.

In the contemporary garden, both rills and canals are a formal way of leading the eye in a specific direction. A canal can contain sufficient perfectly still water to demonstrate exquisite reflections, while a rill may create a lively tension of gushing power within the confines of a stone- or concrete-lined narrow channel.

**below** Sir Geoffrey Jellicoe's Mogul-inspired pools are linked by narrow, descending, grass-edged rills.

**right** In this garden design, wide canals have been used to enclose a central grassed space, and stepping stones make bridges to the island lawn. Ancient olive trees planted in water-tight containers appear to float as if on wild meadow rafts. They are placed at regular intervals along each canal, creating delightful reflections in the still water.

**left** Limestone lines the canal in this city garden. The descending strip of water is flanked by two lines of pleached limes to lead the eye to a Venetian stone wellhead.

**right** A water staircase in which the descent of water is formalized over steps by means of an enclosed canal.

**below** Another example of Sir Geoffrey Jellicoe's inspired water garden, where the square and circular pools and their linking rills have a more formal and distinct border. The border defines the clarity of their shape well into the distance, deliberately leading the focus to rest on the gap in the hedge in order to view the breathtaking landscape beyond the garden.

# water containers

Water can bring life to even the tiniest of gardens, even if this is just a fleet of candles floating on the surface of a shallow bowl or the sound of a gurgling fountain contained inside a rounded pot.

**left** It is possible to introduce a water feature into even the smallest of garden spaces, as this sloping row of white, water-filled dishes shows.

Any watertight, frostproof container is suitable for creating a small water feature and is ideal for areas of raised deck or on roof terraces, where a traditional pond may be impractical. Grey steel bowls in geometric shapes suit modern spaces, while a wide shallow stone or concrete bowl will integrate more easily into an Eastern style. For a more rustic look, there are wooden barrels, available from most garden centres, which come ready-treated against rot.

Cisterns have been used to collect and store water since Roman times, and these boxy shapes work well set against a wall incorporated with a decorative or simple water spout. By means of a pump, water is ejected under pressure then circulated via the reservoir below.

Free-standing stone fonts or troughs, large terracotta bowls or curvaceous urns make instant gardens for miniature waterlilies. Large bowls or pots, which can be bought with a pre-drilled drainage hole, can incorporate a small fountain, whereby the pump sits on a level spot at the bottom with its plastic-coated wire passing through the hole, which is then sealed with silicon. Most small pumps are designed to run off mains electricity.

Plants added to the water in barrels or bowls are best kept in baskets to control their growth and for easier maintenance, and it is best to use rain water in any small planted water feature. Avoid placing container water gardens in a hot spot.

**above** The constant trickle of water from the jug into the bowl in this self-contained water feature provides movement and gentle sound, without the turbulence of a fountain.

**left** A deep and curvaceous stone bowl sprinkled with scented petals may also be decorated with floating candles to create soft and romantic lighting by night.

## *project* container garden

This containerized water feature is ideal for those who do not have enough space for a full-size pool with an adjacent bog garden area. It can be kept outdoors or in a conservatory (porch), depending on the tenderness of the plants you choose.

The choice of plants that can be grown in wet soils is often far more impressive in its diversity than the range of marginal plants available for small pools, providing the keen gardener with a golden opportunity to indulge. A small wet garden may be considered a water feature in its own right, even if it is not associated with an area of clear water.

These steel water containers can be used to create different planting combinations, with aquatic plants in the outer section and moisture-loving plants in the inner section or vice versa. In this way, you can create the effect of a water and bog garden in a small, enclosed courtyard or even in very dry areas.

**above** *Cyperus involucratus* (umbrella grass).

**above** *Eichhornia crassipes* (water hyacinth).

**above** *Pistia stratiotes* (water lettuce).

**above** *Juncus effusus* f. *spiralis* (corkscrew rush).

### Other water plants to grow in a container

| | |
|---|---|
| *Alisma lanceolatum* | *I. laevigata* 'Snowdrift' |
| *Aponogeton distachyos* | *I. laevigata* 'Variegata' |
| *Caltha palustris* | *I. laevigata* 'Weymouth Midnight' |
| *C. palustris* var. *alba* | |
| *C. palustris* var. 'Plena' | *Lobelia* 'Cinnabar Deep Red' |
| *Equisetum scirpoides* | *Mentha cervina* |
| *Houttuynia cordata* | *Menyanthes trifoliata* |
| *H. cordata* 'Chameleon' | *Myosotis scorpioides* |
| | *Nymphoides pellata* |
| *H. cordata* 'Flore Pleno' | *Orontium aquaticum* |
| | *Pontederia cordata* |
| *Iris laevigata* | *Veronica beccabunga* |

**left** Frost-tender *Cyperus involucratus* (umbrella grass) in the inner bog section, with *Eichhornia crassipes* (water hyacinth) and *Pistia stratiotes* (water lettuce) in the water section, are suited to a cool conservatory (porch).

### You will need

2 galvanized metal square containers, 22 x 22cm (8½ x 8½in) and 55 x 55cm (21½ x 21½in), both 38cm (15in) deep

Compost mix: 400g (14oz) controlled-release fertilizer (osmocote) mixed with 100 litres (25 gallons) aquatic compost (soil mix)

Selection of plants for both containers

Pea gravel or alpine grit

Watering can

**1** Place the smaller container inside the larger one. Decide whether you would like to have bog or aquatic plants in the smaller or larger container.

**2** Add the compost mix to the container in which you are growing bog plants. The recipe for the compost mix, which is given in the list of materials, is specially formulated to sustain moisture-loving plants. Fill the container with compost to within 5cm (2in) of the rim.

**3** Create a hole in the compost for the bog plants – in this case the container has been planted with three umbrella grasses (*Cyperus involucratus*). Add more compost and firm in with your fingers.

**4** Add a layer of pea gravel or alpine grit over the surface of the compost. This will act as a mulch, helping to retain valuable water.

**5** Fill the aquatic container with water, using a watering can. Water in the moisture-loving plants in the bog container at the same time.

**6** Float two to three water hyacinths (*Eicchornia crassipes*) on the surface of the water. In the same way, float two to three water lettuces (*Pistia stratiotes*) on the water surface (*inset*).

**above** As an alternative, try *Juncus effusus* f. *spiralis* (corkscrew rush) in the water section, with *Thalia dealbata* and *Baumea rubiginosa* 'Variegata' in the outer bog section.

# swimming pools

Swimming by moonlight or luxuriating in a hot tub are wonderfully sensual

experiences and the most indulgent way of enjoying the sound, sight and

feel of water in the seclusion of your own garden or terrace.

**below** Outside bathing can be enjoyed all year round by combining a swimming pool with a hot tub. The contours of this tub are followed with a rounded brick edging and curved decking walkways.

The restorative and healing powers of spas have been acknowledged for centuries, and hydrotherapy, developed in the 19th century, today remains one of the most popular health treatments. A well-planned and constructed swimming pool is an expensive investment that requires building by experts. After the initial construction, and if it is to be used all year round, it requires continuous maintenance and heating to keep the water fresh and clean and at a comfortable temperature.

In hot climates and where the pool is the inevitable centre of an outdoor lifestyle, it should be sited near the house, where it becomes part of a terrace for sitting, dining and entertaining. Square, rectangular or other formal-shaped pools may be incorporated into the paving near the house, and their geometric lines will naturally follow the angles and contours of the building. Wide expanses of water have a natural affiliation to decking, and a wooden surround dries out better and is softer underfoot than other hard landscaping materials. This needs to be incorporated with a non-slip border to avoid accidents.

The most popular colours for the interior of swimming pools in sunny climates, where the water reflects the almost permanently blue skies, are shades of blue, grey and turquoise, but in a more temperate climate, inky black or dark blue have the effect of creating a mirror, which reflects surrounding buildings or trees.

**right** In the hot summers of Australia many people consider it an essential rather than a luxury to have a swimming pool. This house in Sydney integrates two pools, providing cool water both indoors and outside.

## *case study* seaside bathing

Although set apart from the house, this swimming pool and garden

echo its innovative modern design and fine use of natural materials,

to create an outdoor room for summer entertaining.

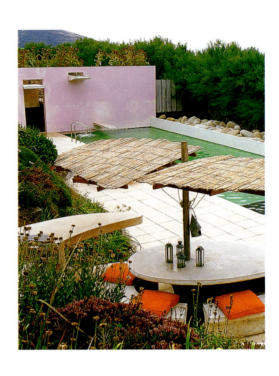

This swimming pool is designed to blend with the award-winning house, which sits on a cliff top with views over the ocean and has windows that wind down into the ground to leave the rooms entirely open to the elements. Reference is made throughout the house to its maritime surroundings, and indigenous materials such as granite, slate and limestone give the house a local context.

Although the house is next to the sea, access to the water is restricted by a steep cliff, so a rectangular swimming pool protected by a dense evergreen hedge provides a secluded and sheltered spot in which the whole family can swim safely. Between the hedge and the pool's retaining wall is a wide border of oversized beach pebbles to give the pool context, and at one end a lilac pink concrete wall creates further screening and conceals the pump and a small changing room. A metal chute juts out from near the top of the screen wall from which a torrent of water cascades. At the opposite end of the pool a semi-submerged walkway divides a shallower area of water from the deep end, and a rectangular area of decking creates easy access to this shallow end.

Protected by the hillside and surrounded by salt-tolerant plants and strong vertical phormium is a circular concrete dining table with a raised and curved food-preparation area and integrated barbecue. Diners are further sheltered by a canopy of bamboo poles, which can be removed in the winter.

**below** Sitting and relaxing close to the sight and sound of water can be more pleasurable than actually bathing, especially if the weather is inclement.

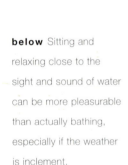

**above** The brightly painted lilac wall at the deep end of this pool offers additional shelter from the wind. It also conceals the pump and changing rooms, and provides a high spot for the metal chute which gushes water alongside the diving board.

**right** The simplicity of this cliff-top swimming pool blends harmoniously with the surrounding landscape. Huge rounded boulders echo the smooth pebbles found on the beach below, and the planting of indigenous, salt-tolerant plants offers protection from the strong sea winds.

# *blueprint* making a formal pool

One of the simplest yet most effective uses of water is a sunken formal pool. The crisp edges of a paving surround frame the water beautifully, particularly in winter when the water is free from foliage and the low sunshine is reflected in its mirror-like surface. A preformed rigid unit is an ideal choice for such a project, eliminating the folds that are necessary when using a flexible liner. If possible, choose a resin-bonded unit rather than a plastic one because its strength helps to compensate for any slight deficiency in the preparation.

**1** As formal pools have a regular shape, their position can be marked out by inverting the preformed unit on the proposed site and marking the outline with canes or sand.

**2** If the pool has a marginal shelf, dig out the whole area to the depth of the shelf.

**3** Rake the soil in the base of the hole so that the deeper zone of the unit will make an impression when it is pressed on the surface.

**4** Dig out the deeper zone indicated by the imprint so that it is 5cm (2in) deeper than the depth of the pool.

**5** After spreading some sand over the base of the hole, place the preformed unit into the excavation and check that the sides are level with a spirit (carpenter's) level on a straight-edged piece of wood. This should be long enough to rest on opposite sides of the pool.

**6** Fill the unit with a few inches of water in order to keep the pool steady and level while firming the soil back around the outside of the preformed unit.

**7** Keep adding a little more water until the pool is almost full. Make a final check on levels and then lay the paving surround to overlap the pool edge by 5cm (2in). The slabs should be mortared on to a foundation of sand or hardcore.

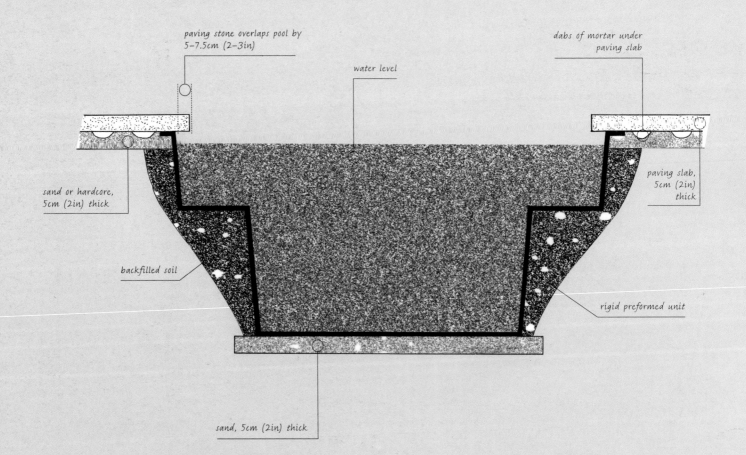

paving stone overlaps pool by 5–7.5cm (2–3in)

dabs of mortar under paving slab

water level

sand or hardcore, 5cm (2in) thick

paving slab, 5cm (2in) thick

backfilled soil

rigid preformed unit

sand, 5cm (2in) thick

# *blueprints* making informal and wildlife pools

The flexibility in shape of an informal pool means that it can be designed to fit any garden size or shape. Flexible liners offer the best value here, enabling last-minute changes to be made to the shape. A skilled designer can produce pleasing effects with the range of edges, such as cobbles and turf, that can be used around informal pools. A wildlife pool can be constructed with a flexible liner in much the same way as an informal pool. It should include a shallow beach to allow for the easy movement of wildlife.

## INFORMAL POOL WITH A BOGGY AREA

**1** Mark the outline of the pool with pegs, and check levels all round.

**2** Dig out the pool to a depth of 23cm (9in) to create marginal shelves, about 30cm (12in) wide, in the case of an informal pool.

**3** Dig out the deeper zone inside to a minimum depth of 45cm (18in). Rake over the surface of the excavation to remove any sharp stones.

**4** Insert an underlay into the excavation and then drape a liner over the whole area,

with an overlap of 30cm (12in) around the edge.

**5** Disguise the edges of the liner with soil, and finish the pool edges. Fill with water.

**6** To create a boggy area, dig a separate hole, 38cm (15in) deep, which is adjacent to the pool. Line the hole with a sheet of plastic, and make one or two slits in it.

**7** Pierce holes along the length of a garden hose and insert a bung into one end. Lay the hose into a layer of gravel on the bottom of the boggy area. Return the soil to the hole.

**8** Attach a female hose connector to the pipe, which should remain poking out of the soil to allow for topping up.

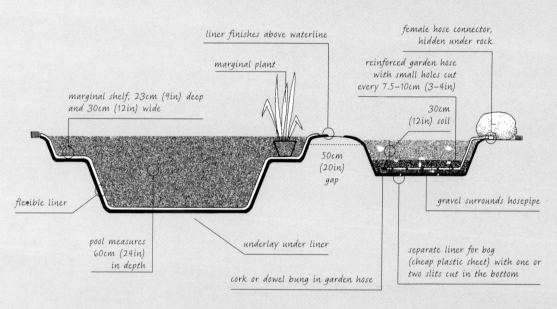

*liner finishes above waterline*

*marginal plant*

*marginal shelf, 23cm (9in) deep and 30cm (12in) wide*

*flexible liner*

*pool measures 60cm (24in) in depth*

*underlay under liner*

*cork or dowel bung in garden hose*

*female hose connector, hidden under rock*

*reinforced garden hose with small holes cut every 7.5–10cm (3–4in)*

*30cm (12in) soil*

*50cm (20in) gap*

*gravel surrounds hosepipe*

*separate liner for bog (cheap plastic sheet) with one or two slits cut in the bottom*

## WILDLIFE POOL

**1** During the excavation, dig out a saucer-shaped pool to a minimum depth of 60cm (24in), ensuring that the gradient of the sides is gentle enough to support a surround of soil or cobbles.

**2** Insert an underlay into the excavation and then drape a flexible liner over the pool area, overlapping

the edge of the pool by 15cm (6in).

**3** Cover the liner with a 10–15cm (4–6in) layer of soil and create a cobble beach to extend from 5–8cm (2–3in) above the waterline to 15–23cm (6–9in) below.

**4** Fill with water, pouring the water on to a slab to reduce soil disturbance.

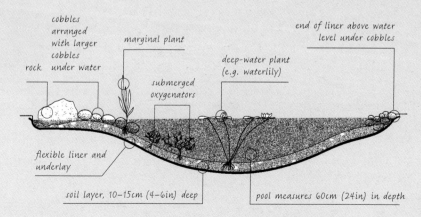

*cobbles arranged with larger cobbles under water*

*rock*

*marginal plant*

*deep-water plant (e.g. waterlily)*

*end of liner above water level under cobbles*

*submerged oxygenators*

*flexible liner and underlay*

*soil layer, 10–15cm (4–6in) deep*

*pool measures 60cm (24in) in depth*

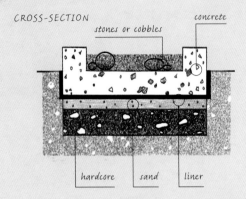

CROSS-SECTION
stones or cobbles
concrete

hardcore    sand    liner

# *blueprint* building a rill or canal

A formal shallow canal or rill has always been a popular method of breaking up areas of a garden or forming the central axis to a symmetrical layout. The long, narrow water surface can look like a thread of mercury, reflecting the sky in designs where all available light is valuable. The source of the rill also provides an opportunity to make an original feature, and in this illustration a stainless-steel pipe makes an emphatic statement in a modern design.

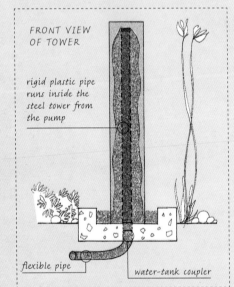

FRONT VIEW
OF TOWER

rigid plastic pipe
runs inside the
steel tower from
the pump

flexible pipe

water-tank coupler

**1** Construct a reservoir that is large enough to contain all the shallow water in the rill at the point where the rill discharges the water. Place a submersible pump in the reservoir and place a paving stone over the top to keep out light and debris.

**2** Construct a shallow, watertight trench using a flexible liner and concrete shuttering along the proposed route of the rill.

**3** Bury a corrugated, flexible delivery pipe at a shallow depth alongside the concrete rill to deliver the water to the source point, in this case a stainless-steel tower. The flexible pipe can either come up behind the tower and join the water-tank coupler or be built into the concrete when the rill is being made, as is shown here. The pipe then joins a rigid pipe at the bottom of the tower.

**4** Connect a rigid plastic pipe inside the steel tower from the coupler to finish just below the top.

**5** When the pump is working the water will fall from inside the rigid pipe and, as the pressure builds up inside the pipe, the rate of flow will become greater from the exit slot at the top, and the water will push out and fall to the rill below

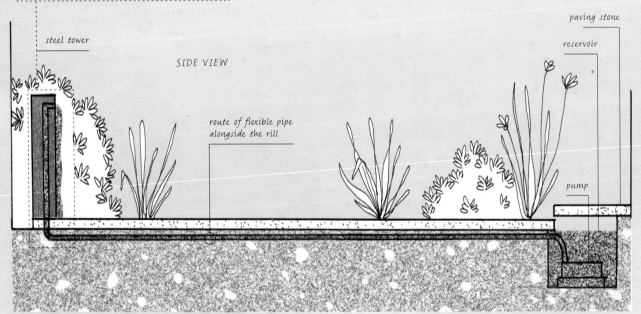

steel tower

SIDE VIEW

route of flexible pipe
alongside the rill

paving stone

reservoir

pump

# *blueprint* building a raised timber pool

A raised pool is not only safer than a sunken pool, which may be a consideration where small children are concerned, but it is also easier to construct in concrete courtyards, for example, where excavation is difficult. If the sides of the pool are substantial, raised pools can also provide seating, adding to the pleasure of viewing the water or the details of the plants at close quarters. Reclaimed railway sleepers (ties) are now readily available and make an ideal surround.

**1** Mark out the shape of the pool on a level surface to dimensions that reduce the need to cut the railway sleepers. Lay a gravel base on the site to increase drainage under the wood.

**2** Put the first course of sleepers in position, and then lay the second and third courses, bonding the sleepers at the corners.

**3** To give the pool extra rigidity, screw right-angle brackets into the inside corners, and knock in long galvanized nails at an angle from one sleeper into the sleeper beneath.

**4** Drape a sheet of plastic over the excavation so that it drapes down the inside edge and across the floor. Secure the plastic with carpet tacks.

**5** Place a rigid preformed unit inside the railway sleepers with the deeper zone bedded on to a 5cm (2in) layer of sand. Backfill with soil or sand into the gap between the unit and the sleepers. Check that the unit is level as the soil is filled around the sides.

**6** Plant the gaps between the rigid unit and the sleepers with carpeting plants such as thyme (*Thymus*) and add flat rocks to disguise the edge of the preform.

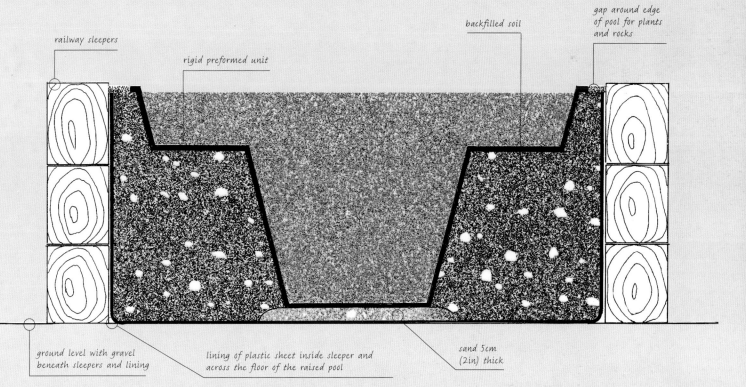

railway sleepers

rigid preformed unit

backfilled soil

gap around edge of pool for plants and rocks

ground level with gravel beneath sleepers and lining

lining of plastic sheet inside sleeper and across the floor of the raised pool

sand 5cm (2in) thick

Water is a highly precious resource, and the very earliest civilizations evolved where there was a supply of fresh water. Indeed, in the ancient world springs were regarded as the source of health and fertility.

The sound of moving water has always been a source of great fascination, and creating an outlet of water, whether in the form of streams, waterfalls and cascades, fountains and jets, or small water features, has been a common practice in many cultures. For example, at Mari, one of the cities of Mesopotamia, a stone figure dating from around 2000 BC portrays a female goddess holding a vase into which water was piped and poured out into a pool. This ancient design is one of the earliest prototype forms of a fountain, symbolizing the source of all life.

**right** Moving water can be created in many ways, whether as a spout, waterfall or fountain. Here, the continual sound of water as it falls from wall-mounted masks into a deep pool is in contrast to the sound of water falling on stones or tiny droplets skittering across a pond.

outlet

Throughout history, the gardens of pleasure were the prerogative of royalty, aristocracy and the fabulously wealthy. Impossibly vast sums of money were used to create artificial lakes and reservoirs, often by diverting water from miles away, to feed the fountains and pools of the grand palazzi and châteaux of Italy and France.

The much-documented excesses of the Roman emperor Nero (AD 37–68) included the creation of opulent gardens with scores of fountains and water features incorporating bizarre water tricks and effects, which appealed to his very eccentric sense of humour. Many were devised by Hero of Alexandria, an engineer who used water pressure to invent hydraulic systems that created water sounds from whistling figures or singing birds. Statues would emit water from nostrils and ears, or were designed to be more erotic or even obscene. These water tricks, or *giochi d'acqua* as they were later known in the Italian Renaissance gardens, exemplified the desire not only to control water on a grand scale but also to add a further dimension of fun and frivolity.

**far left** Water gently cascades down white stone steps into contrasting dark slate-filled pools. The surface is illuminated by the fading rays of a setting sun.

**left** This powerful jet of water, which is bubbling furiously, resembles a natural geyser as it forces its way up a fabricated spout located between the edges of stone paving.

# streams

In essence, a stream is a body of water in constant flow and it

may gently meander between banks of swaying rushes or tumble

down stony outcrops creating scores of tiny cascades.

F ew gardens have the benefit of a natural stream, but with careful planning, design and expert assistance it is possible to create this form of moving water. Informal and natural-looking streams can be integrated into rock gardens or wooded banks by creating a pool or small spring at the top of the slope, with another at the bottom of the stream, from where the water in this reservoir is circulated back to the top by means of a submersible pump. As a general rule, the top pond or source acts as the "header tank", and the bottom pool or mouth of the stream needs to be at least twice as large as the top. The pump must be located at the lowest point of the bottom pond, and its size is dependent on the gradient, shape of the stream bed and volume of water.

Streams that resemble a naturally occurring feature can be a good choice. One option is a mountain stream, characterized by a strong gradient and a rocky bottom. Mountain streams rush down their course, bouncing off rocks and plunging down waterfalls, creating sound and visual excitement. Planting is inevitably restricted to the banks, as the fast-moving torrent carries everything down with it.

A calmer choice would be a softly flowing brook with a low gradient, meandering course and a sandy or pebble bottom. Such a gentle stream, which permits marginal plants to colonize the edges, could emulate those found in English meadows virtually hidden by tall rushes and grasses and the delicate summer flowers of indigenous plants, or it could take inspiration from the Zen gardens of Japan, with huge moss- and lichen-covered boulders, where water slowly trickles and mysteriously disappears and reappears around groves of lush bamboo.

**below** With the constant presence of clean, running water, the banks of a stream will support lush and intensive foliage.

**above** This water garden includes some of the finest examples of naturalistic streams.

**right** Sir Geoffrey Jellicoe's naturalistic series of streams set on a gentle hillside required masterful skill in assessing the drop of each waterfall in relation to the rate of flow. The exquisite sound and sight of each cascade can be appreciated from a series of tiny bridges.

**left** Before creating a
naturalistic stream it is
inspiring to observe the
way completely natural
streams run a softly
undulating course.
Moisture-loving plants
tend to colonize the
shallows on small
outcrops of land, their
green lushness
contrasting with the
smooth, flat grey slate
stones beneath the
surface of the water.

# waterfalls and cascades

The sensual attractions of moving water can be enhanced

dramatically by the addition of a natural waterfall or brimming

water pouring as a perfect sheet over a wide sill.

There is a magical quality to the sound and sight of water tumbling over an outcrop of mossy boulders and the more formal cascade where water falls down a vertical face, creating a wide symmetrical sheet. The design possibilities are endless, and they may be inspired by the natural landscape or take their theme from historical reference.

Natural waterfalls occur down the sides of valleys, where the water cuts its own often irregular path through a series of rocks or boulders, and it is quite a challenging feat of artistry and engineering to create an authentic-looking imitation. In order to look uncontrived, the rocks need to appear to jut out of the water, so their size is determined by how much is needed both above and below the waterline. They may take the form of a series of irregular steps, or you may prefer one single fall.

**left** Among the deep green foliage of a tropical garden, a brightly coloured tiled mosiac surface is highlighted by the cascading water.

**below** A precise horizontal sill ensures a perfect sheet of falling water.

**above** A softly flowing undulating stream partially concealed by overhanging plants is integrated into a pond by means of a small waterfall. The falling water helps to oxygenate the open water.

**right** The formal water staircase is a classic design, with a place in both traditional and contemporary gardens.

Obviously, the greater the fall, the louder the sound, and this element needs to be considered when you are positioning the waterfall. The result of air being mixed in with the flow can create spectacular sprays and a white-water effect, as the gushing torrent breaks over the rocks and boulders in its path.

By contrast, gentle falls create a soft sloping sound, exuding peaceful tranquillity, particularly if they are connected to a series of rock pools, where the virtually still water presents opportunities for marginal planting.

Whichever type of fall you choose, you should never underestimate the sheer power of water, and the construction may require a professional expert to ensure that the installation is both safe and secure with the correct pumps and size of reservoirs. The construction must also take into account how the feature both looks and functions when the circulating system is turned off. To store the water when the pump is not running, the lower pool or underground reservoir needs to accommodate the volume of water in the stream, or it may very well flood the garden.

While copying nature is appropriate in informal settings, a more formal approach has a greater appeal in contemporary gardens or where moving water is desired in closer proximity to a house. Formal falls and symmetrical cascades of water may be incorporated into the changes of level from, say, a terrace to a lower part of the garden.

In the Mogul gardens of Kashmir, stone channels were used to carry water through the descent from one terrace to another, and a series of steps was constructed at a precise angle so as to reflect as much sunlight as possible. The concept of the water staircase, or the *catena d'acqua*, literally "chain of water", which was developed and perfected during the Italian Renaissance, involved bodies of water channelled down the centre of either steps or an architectural ramp.

A formal arrangement of any straight and symmetrical materials, such as concrete, polished stone or metal sills, will cause a uniform flow of water that can be adjusted to create lines of drops falling over the edge or, with a higher flow, a smooth sheet of a length dependent on the height of the fall. As with a natural-looking waterfall, the longer the fall, the greater the sound as the water reaches its destination.

## case study modern cascade

Inspired by the Islamic tradition of an enclosed garden, this courtyard

utilizes modern engineering to create a smooth cascade, the calm

tranquillity of which is enhanced by night-scented plants.

**left** A path of highly polished blue-grey granite flanked with scented plants leads the eye to the illuminated hollow bronze water-sculpture. The sculpture is the focal point of the garden at night.

The design of this garden is partly inspired by the traditional *chahar bagh* or quartered designs of the early Islamic gardens, but also takes historical reference from the Victorian idea of a walled garden, which created a microclimate suitable for non-hardy plants. The garden is designed around numerous walkways of highly polished blue-grey granite. On either side of the central walkway are two identical cascades of water, which fall in symmetrical sheets over silver metal fins. The granite is so reflective it is almost impossible to see where the water ends and the stone begins. Shorter versions of these fins are used to create a louvred panel screen that protects the central part of the garden from the hot sun during the day. Solar or manually driven, this screen permits light to filter through the panels when open, but at night the protective canopy ensures a pleasant environment for evening dining.

At the far end of the central path is a hollow bronze sculptural water feature, dramatically lit from beneath to create the main focus of attention. Evening light is also enhanced by the intensity of solely white plants in formal beds edging the central axis. Lavender hedges and banks of exotic gardenia follow the lines of the water cascades, while formal parterres, edged with rounded balls of box, are filled with ground-covering white petunias. Huge, shallow, granite bowls are planted with lime-white hydrangeas.

**above** The highly polished surface of the granite reflects the trees and plants around the water. It is very difficult to see where the surface ends and the water begins.

**left** A silvery metal louvred panel, identical to that used to make the sun screen above, creates a smooth curved step over which the water slides in a single and perfect sheet.

## *project* caribbean cascade

This dramatic cascade would be suitable for a large garden, particularly in association with a selection of architectural plants such as gunnera, cannas and ferns to create a tropical ambience. You can choose a range of moisture-lovers. Select bright colours to create an exotic effect.

This is an ambitious project in that it involves the excavation and construction of a large base pool, a rocky cascade and a small header pool. The water is circulated by means of a submersible pump from the base pool to the top of the cascade into the header pool. From the header pool, it falls over the edge of the cascade. The base pool at the foot of the cascade is about 6m (20ft) across, which means that you will need a garden of a fairly substantial size to accommodate such a feature.

**above** Choose plants such as *Cyperus papyrus* (giant reed, Egyptian paper reed), *Ligularia* 'The Rocket' and *Lilium regale* for maximum colour.

**left** Moisture-loving plants, such as ferns and candelabra primulas, as well as cannas with their large leaves, create a Caribbean atmosphere around this informal pool.

**right** The water pours over the spillstone to produce a tumbling cascade, creating a cool, calm oasis. The cascade is surrounded by lush planting, including *Cyperus involucratus* (umbrella grass).

**below** Cannas are available in a variety of bright colours, ideal for creating a tropical effect.

### You will need

| | | |
|---|---|---|
| Pegs and string or white spray paint for marking out | Mortaring trowel | Biological filter |
| Spade | Rake | Ultraviolet clarifier |
| Sand | Underlay | Garden hose |
| Sheet of plastic | 1–2 flexible liners | Outdoor connection point |
| Straight-edged piece of wood | Bricks or heavy stones | Electricity supply (circuit breaker) |
| Spirit (carpenter's) level | Submersible pump suitable for a pond measuring 6 x 6m (20 x 20ft), 45cm (18in) deep and with 40cm (16in) wide marginal shelves | Selection of suitable plants, including oxygenators, deep-water aquatics, marginal plants and moisture-loving plants |
| 4 large plastic crates | | |
| 5–6 railway sleepers (ties), 3m (10ft) in length | | |
| 8 tonnes (26 tons) natural rock | Plastic delivery pipe, 2.5cm (1in) in diameter | Turf, bark or paving slabs for edging pool |
| Ready-mix mortar | 10 sandbags | |
| | Large, flat spillstone | |

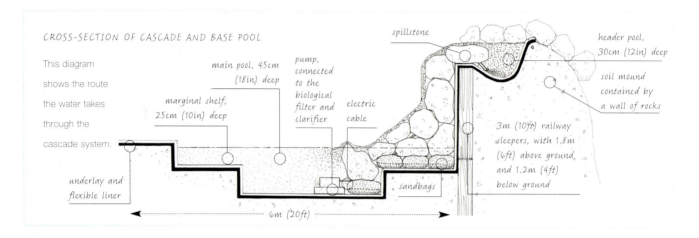

**CROSS-SECTION OF CASCADE AND BASE POOL**

This diagram shows the route the water takes through the cascade system.

*main pool, 45cm (18in) deep*

*marginal shelf, 25cm (10in) deep*

*pump, connected to the biological filter and clarifier*

*electric cable*

*spillstone*

*header pool, 30cm (12in) deep*

*soil mound contained by a wall of rocks*

*3m (10ft) railway sleepers, with 1.8m (6ft) above ground, and 1.2m (4ft) below ground*

*underlay and flexible liner*

*sandbags*

*6m (20ft)*

**1** Choose the site for the cascade carefully; it is preferable if the cascade is south- or west-facing. Mark out the position and shape of the base pool using the pegs and string or spray paint. Dig out the base pool to an initial depth of 25cm (10in). Mark the position of the marginal shelves, which should be 40cm (16in) wide, by sprinkling a line of sand around the inside edge of the pool. Dig out the pool by a further 20cm (8in) so that the final depth is 45cm (18in). Keep the excavated soil on a sheet of plastic because you will need it later to build the cascade. Check levels with a straight-edged piece of wood and a spirit level.

**2** Mound up some sand in the corners of the pool, burying the four crates within the mounds of soil. These will give added strength to the corner contours.

**3** *(left)* The cascade should be approximately 1.8m (6ft) in height. It is fed by a header pool that is raised above ground level on top of a mound of soil. This soil mound should be contained at the back with a wall of rocks and in the front with railway sleepers. Bury five or six sleepers at the front of the cascade to a depth of 1.2m (4ft).

**4** *(right)* Using the soil excavated from the base pool, build up the mound of soil behind the sleepers. Keep the soil in place with a wall of large rocks mortared on top of each other. Create a header pool at the top of the soil mound, 30cm (12in) deep and approximately 90cm (3ft) across.

**5** Rake the excavated area level and remove any sharp objects, such as stones and tree roots. Lay the underlay over the base pool, taking it up and over the front of the cascade and into the header pool. Ensure that the underlay overlaps the sides of the base pool by approximately 15cm (6in). Cover the underlay with one or two flexible liners. Weigh down the edges of the liner with bricks or heavy stones to prevent them from being blown back into the hole. Install the submersible pump at the bottom of the pool by the edge of the marginal shelf under the cascade and run the plastic delivery pipe from the pump to the top of the header pool.

**6** With the pipework in place, you can now build up a wall of rocks to disguise the sleepers and so create the rocky cascade. Place the largest stones at the base of the cascade, using sandbags as a support in order to protect the liner. You will need to mortar a large, flat stone to act as a spillstone on top of the sleepers at the front of the cascade (*see inset, above*). The spillstone can be mortared directly on top of the liner. Build up the surrounding rocks one by one, mortaring them into place with the cement around the header pool and spillstone.

**7** Connect up the biological filter and ultraviolet clarifier, which are vital for keeping the pool clean. The water should run through lengths of delivery pipe from the pump to the ultraviolet clarifier, then from the clarifier to the biological filter before it enters the header pool. Fill the base pool with water and turn on the pump to test the flow of water. Adjust the flow regulator on the pump until you are satisfied with the cascade.

**8** Stock the pool with a good selection of plants. Most aquatic plants can be grown in special aquatic baskets. Plant the marginals on the pond shelves, the deep-water aquatics in the pond (supported by bricks until the plants have grown sufficiently to float on the surface), and the moisture-lovers in the moist soil around the pond edges. Trim off any excess flexible liner and finish the edges of the base pool with turf, bark or paving.

# wall-mounted features

Water features that are mounted against a wall are perfect for a small

courtyard garden. They may take the form of traditional mascarons, or wall

masks, or more modern sheets or spouts of water.

The concept of a wall-mounted fountain or spout originates from the times when domestic water was supplied to many local communities by a central well, and natural springs were utilized to provide public access to fresh drinking water. Spouts conveyed water via pipes through a wall, where a stone bowl built below the outlet caught the water, thus providing a basin for washing the hands and face at a comfortable level – the precursor of today's hand basin. Many contemporary bathroom designers are now reverting back to this ancient design in preference to the traditional Victorian pre-moulded bowls with integrated taps. Similarly, modern gardens with formally shaped basins or pools are best served with a simple wall-mounted spout or sill rather than something more elaborate.

**below** Water falls from a horizontal copper pipe beneath a black-slate-topped pillar and slides down a sheet of clear Perspex (Plexiglass) into a raised reservoir filled with slate paddle stone.

In Italian Renaissance gardens, wall masks, often cast in metal or carved in stone and depicting strange and often grotesque faces, were used to feed a dipping-well: a small basin or pool, possibly raised, set against a retaining wall and above which a vaulted arch partially covered the reservoir below. Such features were either self-contained or allowed the water to overflow the pool or basin, feeding into a rill or canal that conducted the water to other features. The dipping-well was one of Sir Edwin Lutyens' favourite water features, and there are some fine examples of his designs at Hestercombe House in Somerset, England.

Less ambitious and smaller features are the completely self-contained set pieces that integrate the pump, outlet and basin, which require little more than fixing to a suitable wall and connecting the cable to an exterior socket (outlet). It is worth first observing such features in action, as the sound effects may not be desirable, and often the sound of the pump can drown any noise that the water may make.

**left** This striking mascaron or wall mask is a modern interpretation of a feature used extensively in the water gardens of the Italian Renaissance, where the spouting water was collected in pools, stone basins or dipping-wells.

**above** The wall-mounted spout is an alternative to the fountain from which water is poured rather than forced out under pressure into a small pool or canal. It is an ideal design for small spaces and windy sites.

## *case study* rooftop waterfall

City rooftops can be very hot, dry and windswept places,

but with windbreaks, screens and the refreshing sound of

water, they can make an urban oasis.

O n an urban rooftop, measuring just 10 x 20m (30 x 60ft), a perfect outside room has been created high above the city. By integrating straight lines with gentle curves, the designers have made an uncomplicated space full of visual movement with places for both plants and people. This is a calming garden retreat, ideal for relaxing away from the noise and rush of the streets below.

Between the silvery grey iroko decking and the sandy coloured paint-washed walls, which are topped with wind-permeable fencing, is the seating area. Here, striking galvanized steel containers and benches are shaded by huge canvas sails suspended between the top of the fencing and a huge, mast-like pole, giving the rooftop a nautical theme.

Opposite the seating area is a tall galvanized metal plinth set against a maroon-painted wall, from which a small sill resembling an open letter box provides the outlet for a smooth sheet of water, which falls into a narrow, right-angled, steel-lined rill. On one side of the rill is a small asymmetrical planting pocket, mass planted with *Ophiopogon planiscapus* 'Nigrescens', a well-behaved perennial evergreen grass with dramatic black strappy leaves and pinkish blue flowers in summer.

Other planting echoes the nautical theme of the garden, with containers of the huge *Cynara cardunculus* (cardoon), *Pennisetum alopecuroides* (fountain grass), a tree, *Tamarix gallica* (tamarisk) and blue *Agapanthus*. The plants were deliberately

**below** At night, the calm and cool atmosphere is dramatically changed. The gushing water is theatrically lit by two powerful uplighters at the bottom of the rill, creating the impression that the red-painted wall is on fire.

**above** The narrow rill of still water is designed to exactly mirror the image of the galvanized steel pillar, with its gaping mouth and sheet of clear cooling water.

chosen to withstand the tough growing conditions, which are similar to those found in windy seaside gardens, and the drying atmosphere, typical of rooftops, is alleviated by the installation of a computer-operated irrigation system.

All the containers and planting pockets are illuminated by night and cast active shadows against the colourwashed walls. A light source situated at the bottom of the rill and angled to shine through the falling water appears to make the surrounding maroon wall glow like fire at night, and the galvanized plinth reflects light back across the decking. This magical lighting display and the cooling effect of the water on a hot day make this a favourite part of the rooftop garden.

**above** The simplicity of the silvery grey decking and galvanized steel bench contrasts with the powerful design of the water feature. The strong angles of the rill and the steel pillar are emphasized, set against the deep red wall.

# fountains, jets and spouts

The sound and sight of water falling on stones or into a pool can

produce an energetic exuberance or exude a soothing and cooling

atmosphere, creating a pleasant humidity for both plants and people.

Probably the most important architectural and engineering water feature in any garden, whether Eastern or Western, is the fountain. Throughout history the most successful and certainly the most impressive fountains have been supplied by water powered entirely by gravity rather than by any artificial means. They can be loosely divided into two categories – those decorated with sculpture and those where the movement and play of water is the major attraction. Figurative sculpture was prohibited by the text in the Koran, so Islamic gardens like those at the Alhambra and Generalife in Spain's Granada feature very simple fountains, where the patterns of water and the interplay of the jets create the decorative effect.

Electrically operated submersible and surface pumps now produce the power for moving water artificially, and the size and style of pump depends primarily on the desired spray height, which should be no more than the diameter of the pool.

The slightest breeze can blow the spray sideways and out of the reservoir, possibly emptying the pool completely. For spray heights up to about 1.2m (4ft), a low-voltage submersible pump is suitable, and for heights up to 2.4m (8ft) a mains submersible is adequate. Multiple fountains and single jets over 2.4m (8ft) will probably need a mains surface pump. There is a wide range of fountain heads, which produce jets of differing configurations, and most may be adjusted to change the effects. It is vital to ensure that the pump is both frostproof and quiet while running, and it must be installed on a completely level surface. Alternatively, a pump can be used to circulate water from a spout attached to a wall or any other vertical surface.

**below** Movement and sound are created by the simplest of metal water spouts gushing into the centre of this naturalistic pool. Ripples are sent to the pebbled shoreline, lapping against the stone lined edge.

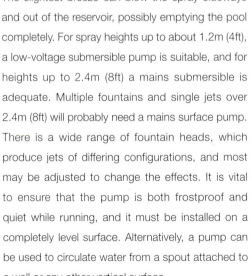

**above** A single frothy jet projects through the decorative metal grille covering this formal pool. The grille also functions as an unobtrusive safety feature.

**right** The parasol shape of this small fountain creates the gentlest of sounds and the smallest of movements, so as not to disturb the flowers and pads of the floating white waterlilies.

**left** The box hedging in this intricate maze, with its backdrop of symmetrically placed trees, is broken up by the regularly spaced water spouts which shoot up playfully along the sides and in the centre. The beech hedging that surrounds the whole garden provides an enclosed space in which to relax, as well as a welcome sense of privacy.

# *project* bird-bath fountain

This bold, sculptural water feature is perfect for a formal garden and could be used as a focal point at the end of a vista or within a terrace area. Alternatively, its strong form would work well within or next to a formal reflective pond. This feature would also suit an intimate space, perhaps situated in a corner and surrounded by foliage plants. Locating the feature in a cool, shady spot will encourage a layer of soft green moss to grow on the outside faces of the concrete troughs.

The water has a number of qualities, including the bubbling jet at the top, the surface tension as it brims at the edge and the gentle cascade down the face of the stones. The feature can be easily adjusted by increasing or decreasing the flow. You can also create different effects with pebbles and other materials to disrupt the flow from the exit pipe at the top; this creates a number of varied sounds and thus different moods.

**far left, above and below** Water bubbles up and into the concrete basin, sliding down the sides of each trough until it reaches the base reservoir. The water is recirculated back up to the basin through the pump. Tiny aquatic lights bring the fountain to life at night.

## You will need

| | |
|---|---|
| Spade | Plastic hose, 19mm (¾in) in diameter |
| Spirit (carpenter's) level | Concrete basin to act as a lid |
| Straight-edged length of wood | Submersible pump, maximum flow 1980l (520 gallons) per hour |
| Plastic reservoir tank, approximately 60cm (24in) in diameter and 60cm (24in) deep | 25mm (1in) galvanized metal grille |
| Geotextile fleece | Wirecutters |
| Sharp knife | Fine plastic shade netting |
| Plastic flexible liner | Cobbles, rocks and gravel |
| Garden hose | Electricity supply (circuit breaker) |
| Electric drill and 25mm (1in) drill bit | Foliage plants to surround and soften the water feature |
| 3 concrete troughs, approximately 45 x 45 x 45cm (18 x 18 x 18in) | Chemical product to keep the feature free from algal growth |

**1** Clear and level an area approximately 180sq cm (28sq in) to a depth of about 5cm (2in), with sloping sides. Within the cleared area, dig a hole approximately 60cm (24in) by 60cm (24in). Ask an electrician to dig a trench for the power supply for which you will need an outdoor socket (outlet) or waterproof junction box. Insert the plastic reservoir tank in the hole.

**2** Check that the reservoir is level using a spirit level on a straight-edged piece of wood. Line the cleared area and reservoir with geotextile fleece. Using a sharp knife, cut a hole in the fleece above the reservoir.

**3** Lay the flexible liner over the fleece and the reservoir. Gradually add water to the reservoir in order to pull the liner into place, remembering to carefully fold the liner flat over the cleared area.

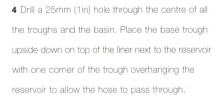

**4** Drill a 25mm (1in) hole through the centre of all the troughs and the basin. Place the base trough upside down on top of the liner next to the reservoir with one corner of the trough overhanging the reservoir to allow the hose to pass through.

**5** (*left*) Feed the hose from the reservoir through the hole in the base trough, then slide the two other troughs, one at a time, down the hose until each trough is sitting square on top of the one below. Complete the tower by placing the concrete basin on top of the upper trough.

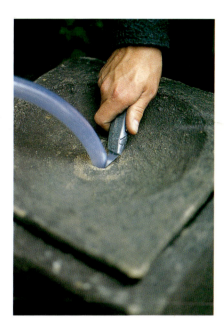

**6** Cut away the excess hose with a sharp knife, so that it is flush with the basin. Connect the pump to the hose and place in the reservoir. Cover with the galvanized metal grille. Cut out the corner of the grille with wirecutters to fit around the base trough. Cover the grille with fine plastic shade netting.

**7** Cover the netting and liner with cobbles, rocks and gravel. Fill the system with water, turn on the power and adjust the flow of water as required. Evaporation will soon reduce the water supply, but the reservoir can be topped up easily by pouring water through the cobbles until the water can be seen at the lowest point. You can also top up the fountain from above, as shown.

**8** Surround the finished fountain with lush foliage plants such as *Fatsia japonica* (castor oil plant) and a selection of ferns. To keep the feature and surrounding cobbles free from algal growth, use one of the chemical products designed for recirculating water features, which are harmless to aquatic wildlife. Follow the manufacturer's instructions carefully.

# small water features

Virtually every style of water feature can be scaled down to provide

a fascinating source of attraction, a sensory experience of sound

and movement, or the silent peace of beautiful light and reflections.

Small-scale water features can make a major impact because they can incorporate so many desirable sensory elements often lacking in tiny outdoor spaces. In fact, small features can be more effective and practical than those on a large scale. For example, a small hot tub with stimulating spa jets for muscle-soothing hydrotherapy may prove to be far more popular than a full-size swimming pool, and for a fraction of the cost. Equally, as an alternative to a pond or raised pool, a tiny bubble fountain gurgling up between a bed of rounded pebbles is both easy to install and requires little maintenance, while also creating a humid microclimate for lush-leaved plants and the safest option for homes with small children or imminent plans for a family.

Small spaces need meticulous planning, and the scale and detail of a water feature must be considered in the context of the overall garden design. For instance, a highly decorative and traditional stone wall mask will look out of place in a modern setting, which is better suited to a simple copper spout or a wide polished marble sill.

Any water feature will inevitably become the focal point in a small space, and this element is the first consideration at the planning stage. Still water relaxes, while gushing water in a confined space may just be too alarming, particularly if accompanied by dramatic sound effects.

**left** An elegantly tiered feature of four slate tiles with a fountain designed to be plugged in, filled up and switched on.

**above** By pumping water through a hollowed rock plinth, this polished marble hydrosphere is set on a continually spinning motion.

**left** Tiny springs often emerge from beneath a rocky basin and this natural feature can be created with a pre-drilled piece of stone through which water is pumped from a sunken reservoir.

## *project* mosaic bowl

This striking water feature is perfect for use outdoors on a patio or indoors in a conservatory (porch). Being portable, it can be brought in and out of the garden and would make a perfect centrepiece (and talking point) on a summer evening. The brightly coloured tiles are beautifully enhanced by the exotic setting, which is created by the surrounding planting. The whole feature evokes a warm tropical night, spent relaxing and listening to the gentle trickle of the water as it falls back into the bowl.

**above** A tropical effect is achieved by choosing a harmonious colour palette of purple, red, pink, orange and yellow opaque glass tiles to line the bowl.

**left** Guzmanias have a bright red or orange, star-shaped bract that produces small white or yellow, short-lived flowers. They are ideal plants for creating a lush, exotic effect.

**left** Bromeliads are distinguished by their bold foliage and showy flowers, such as the rich and tropical colours of this *Guzmania lingulata* 'Major' and *Ananas bracteatus* 'Tricolor', a variety of the red pineapple.

### You will need

| | |
|---|---|
| Circular wooden panel, slightly smaller than the reservoir | Electric drill |
| Small dustbin (trash can) to act as a reservoir, about 60cm (24in) in diameter and 75cm (30in) deep | Selection of glass mosaic tiles in a range of rich tropical colours |
| | Piece of paper |
| Screws | Tile nippers |
| Screwdriver | Goggles |
| 4 wheeled feet | Fibreglass bowl with a 20mm (¾in) hole drilled in centre |
| 4 wooden blocks | |
| Hammer | |
| 5cm (2in) length of copper pipe, 2cm (¾in) in diameter | Copper spraypaint |
| | Tile adhesive |
| White plastic container | Grout |
| Small pump, 4 litres (1 gallon) per minute | Grout spreader |
| | Cloth |
| | Electricity supply (circuit breaker) |

**1** Fix the wooden panel inside the reservoir by screwing through from the outside of the dustbin. Attach the wheeled feet to the blocks of wood and screw the wooden blocks to the underside of the wooden panel (*see inset, above*).

**2** Using a hammer, flatten the piece of copper pipe at one end in order to create a narrow jet of water. Using the tip of a screwdriver (*see inset*), open up the flattened end of the copper pipe slightly to ensure that the water will flow freely.

**3** Position the white container in the centre of the reservoir. Add the pump, threading the cable through a pre-drilled hole in the side of the reservoir at the base.

**4** Select the glass tiles in a range of colours to achieve a bold, brightly coloured effect.

**5** (*left*) It is a good idea to test out the design on a piece of paper first. Arrange the tiles in concentric circles to achieve a pleasing blend of colours.

**6** (*right*) If necessary, cut the tiles into halves using the tile nippers. Wear protective goggles when cutting.

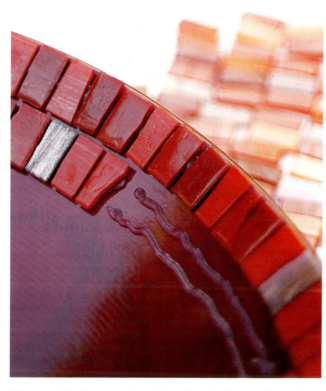

**7** Spray the outside of the fibreglass bowl with copper paint if desired. Starting at the rim of the bowl, apply two lines of tile adhesive, keeping a small gap between the lines.

**8** Press each tile firmly on to the adhesive. When the first row of tiles is in place, follow the same procedure for the second row, and continue with each row until you reach the centre.

**9** Finish by laying the final circle of tiles in the centre of the dish. You may have to cut the tiles to fit the final row. Remember to wear the protective goggles when cutting. Allow to dry. Grout between the tiles using the grout spreader. Allow to dry, then wipe clean with a damp cloth. Fill the white container with water and place the bowl over the copper pipe.

**10** Adjust the flow rate of the pump to create a range of different sounds, from a gushing fountain to a gentle trickle, depending on your mood.

# *blueprint* making a stream and waterfall system

The design and construction of an informal stream and waterfall system offers endless opportunities. Although there are preformed stream units available, which simplify construction, the use of a flexible liner and a variety of rocks makes for a more natural-looking cascade where the width of the stream and waterfalls can vary. By placing the edging rocks on the liner and filling with soil behind them to the height of the liner edge, wet areas can be created for streamside aquatics.

**1** Mark out the direction and width of the stream with canes, identifying where any waterfalls will be positioned.

**2** Dig out the stream to a depth of 20–23cm (8–9in) in a series of steps. Rake over and remove any sharp edges.

**3** Starting from the marginal shelf in the bottom pool, drape the liner along the route of the stream, ensuring that there is enough liner to incorporate the vertical steps and sides where the liner will be tucked up behind rocks along the streamside.

**4** With the liner loosely in place, place a foundation stone on the marginal shelf of the bottom pool to act as a support for a flat waterfall spillstone on top.

**5** Make a fold in the liner behind the spillstone to prevent water seeping under the stone. Place rocks at

the side of the spillstone so that the water is directed over the flat stone. Mortar the gaps between the rocks to ensure a waterproof seal.

**6** Place rocks either side of the stream, ensuring there is adequate liner outside the rocks so that the liner can be lifted into a vertical position above the water-line. Hold the edges of the liner in place with soil.

**7** Repeat this process up the stream until you reach the top. Create a small pool to receive the water from a buried pipe that runs from the pump in the base pool.

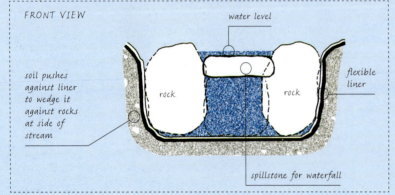

FRONT VIEW

water level

soil pushes against liner to wedge it against rocks at side of stream

rock          rock

flexible liner

spillstone for waterfall

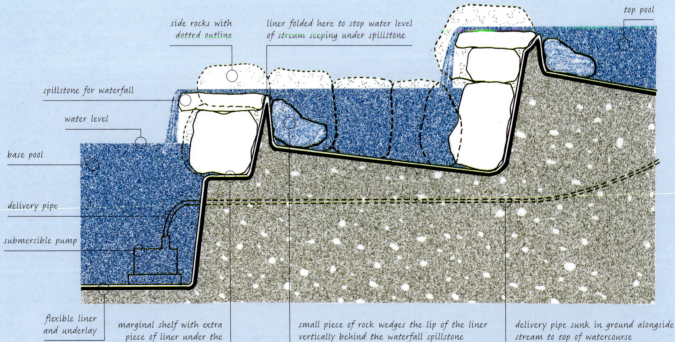

side rocks with dotted outline

liner folded here to stop water level of stream seeping under spillstone

top pool

spillstone for waterfall

water level

base pool

delivery pipe

submersible pump

flexible liner and underlay

marginal shelf with extra piece of liner under the foundation stone

small piece of rock wedges the lip of the liner vertically behind the waterfall spillstone

delivery pipe sunk in ground alongside stream to top of watercourse

# *blueprints* constructing wall fountains

Wall fountains make excellent use of space in a small garden. Most wall fountains have a spout in the form of a mask or gargoyle. The simple wall fountain shown here uses trellis to hide the pipework and a cobble fountain to form the base. This eliminates any green water in the reservoir pool. The more complex fountain shown below has a raised base pool and an intermediate spill basin.

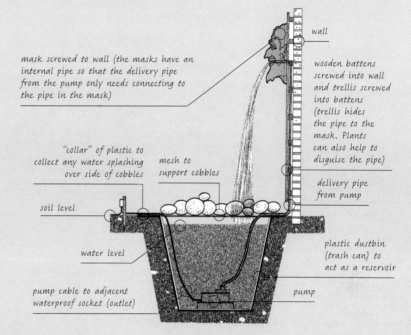

*mask screwed to wall (the masks have an internal pipe so that the delivery pipe from the pump only needs connecting to the pipe in the mask)*

*wall*

*wooden battens screwed into wall and trellis screwed into battens (trellis hides the pipe to the mask. Plants can also help to disguise the pipe)*

*"collar" of plastic to collect any water splashing over side of cobbles*

*mesh to support cobbles*

*delivery pipe from pump*

*soil level*

*water level*

*plastic dustbin (trash can) to act as a reservoir*

*pump cable to adjacent waterproof socket (outlet)*

*pump*

## SIMPLE WALL FOUNTAIN

**1** Screw a suitable mask to the wall at a height of approximately 1.8m (6ft).

**2** Screw wooden battens (laths), 45cm (18in) apart horizontally, on to the wall to the height of the mask. The battens should be a minimum of 2.5cm (1in) thick.

**3** Fix trellis to the battens using screws from ground level to the height of the mask.

**4** Make a hole in the ground at the base of the wall under the mask that is large enough to accommodate a plastic dustbin (trash can) with a plastic collar. There should also be a saucer-shaped area around the dustbin to collect any wind-blown spray from the spout.

**5** Place a pump in the dustbin, and thread a delivery pipe from the pump behind the trellis. Secure the pipe at the back of the mask with a hoseclip.

**6** Cover the dustbin with a galvanized metal mesh and cover this with cobbles. Fill with water and connect the pump to a waterproof socket (outlet).

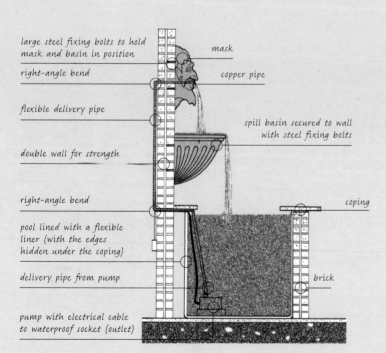

*large steel fixing bolts to hold mask and basin in position*

*mask*

*right-angle bend*

*copper pipe*

*flexible delivery pipe*

*spill basin secured to wall with steel fixing bolts*

*double wall for strength*

*right-angle bend*

*coping*

*pool lined with a flexible liner (with the edges hidden under the coping)*

*delivery pipe from pump*

*brick*

*pump with electrical cable to waterproof socket (outlet)*

## WALL FOUNTAIN WITH A SPILL BASIN AND RAISED POOL BASE

**1** Thread the delivery pipe from the pump in the raised pool through and behind a double wall. Connect the pipe from the pump and the copper pipe in the mask to the pipe behind the wall with right-angle bends.

**2** Secure the mask and the spill basin to the wall with large steel fixing bolts. The distance between the mask and the basin and between the basin and the pool should be equal.

**3** Build the raised pool base by mortaring together a double-thickness brick wall. Contact a qualified bricklayer if necessary.

**4** Line the pool with a flexible liner, taking the ends over the top of the wall by 15cm (6in). Secure the ends by mortaring the coping on top of the liner.

**5** Fill the pool with water and connect the pump to a waterproof socket (outlet).

# *blueprint* building a fountain pool

One of the most exhilarating water features must be a spray fountain, particularly when sunshine sparkles through the spray. Such a scheme may seem quite ambitious at first, but combined with a self-assembly raised pool, no excavation is necessary. There are also endless variations possible in the choice of fountain shape. The main limitation is to contain the height of the fountain to no higher than the diameter of the pond, otherwise it will be out of proportion and there is a risk of losing too much water in windy weather.

**1** Site the raised pool at a point where it can be seen easily from the windows of the house or patio, and have a plain background to the viewpoint.

**2** Prepare a level site; a lawn or paving will be adequate provided the sides of the wooden surround are level.

**3** Assemble the surround as directed in the manufacturer's instructions. Check that the tops of the sides are completely level.

**4** Insert the flexible liner supplied with the self-assembly pool kit. Before stapling the liner to the underside of the pool rim, thread the pump cable between the liner and the wooden surround so that it emerges at ground level at the bottom of the pool wall for connection.

**5** Fill the pool with water and connect the pump using the flow regulator supplied with the pump in order to regulate the force of the fountain.

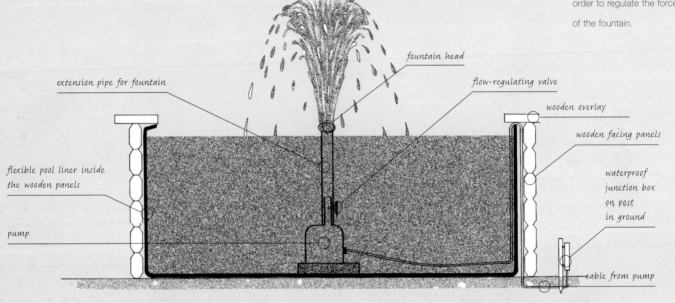

extension pipe for fountain

fountain head

flow-regulating valve

wooden overlay

wooden facing panels

flexible pool liner inside the wooden panels

waterproof junction box on post in ground

pump

cable from pump

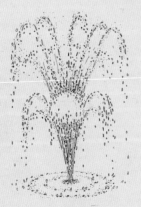

*Multi-tier: ideal for underlighting*

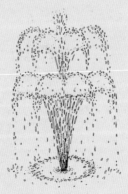

*Plume spray: good for a formal setting*

*Surface rose jet: the simplest spray, often supplied with the pump*

*Bell jet: not very good in windy locations*

# *blueprint* making a drilled rock fountain

There are several innovative variations to a basic cobble fountain, which allow you to use rocks, urns, millstones and other receptacles to tip water back into a hidden reservoir. Cobble fountains can be incorporated into any style or size of garden and offer a maintenance-free water feature that can be turned on and off as required. Our illustration shows how a cobble surround can be adapted to incorporate a piece of rock that has been drilled to allow the water to spill over the sides and enhance its colour.

**1** Dig out a hole for the reservoir, 1m (3ft) square and 45cm (18in) deep.
**2** Line the hole with a flexible liner, allowing for an overlap of 15cm (6in) all around the hole.
**3** If the drilled rock is too heavy to be supported by a standard galvanized metal

mesh, place two supporting bars across the hole from side to side.
**4** Place the pump in the hole on a shallow plinth. Attach a flexible pipe to the pump long enough to be threaded through the galvanized metal mesh. (If you were constructing a simple cobble fountain, then a rigid pipe would replace the flexible pipe from the pump.) Place the piece of galvanized mesh over the top of the reservoir.

**5** Insert a rigid copper pipe into the drilled rock so that it protrudes slightly from the bottom. Connect the delivery pipe from the pump to the copper pipe with a pipe connector.
**6** Fill the reservoir with water and disguise the mesh with a layer of cobbles. Connect the pump to the electrical supply (circuit breaker) and adjust the flow of the pump as required.

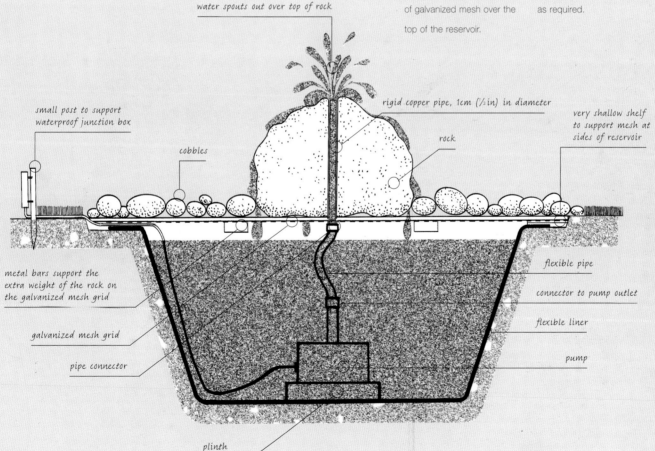

water spouts out over top of rock

rigid copper pipe, 1cm (½in) in diameter

small post to support waterproof junction box

cobbles

rock

very shallow shelf to support mesh at sides of reservoir

metal bars support the extra weight of the rock on the galvanized mesh grid

flexible pipe

connector to pump outlet

galvanized mesh grid

flexible liner

pipe connector

pump

plinth

Water is an essential element in a garden for both plants and people, and while its decorative effect may be considered at a later stage, its installation, whether as an outlet or reservoir, is best planned at the initial design stages. The advantage of new materials and technology is that they permit us to control and contain water in virtually any manner; nevertheless, the less attractive elements of pipework and ducting need careful concealment for a perfectly finished impression. Additional decorative elements such as sensitive lighting and imaginative sculptural effects can enhance the impact of a well-designed water feature while the more structural elements such as bridges, stepping stones and glass panels can create the vital link between moving water and solid land.

**right** Contemporary materials such as stained and coloured concrete, metallic acrylic paints and finishes, and recycled crushed-glass mulches are exciting new developments in the design of modern water features, as are the ingenious innovations in pump technology.

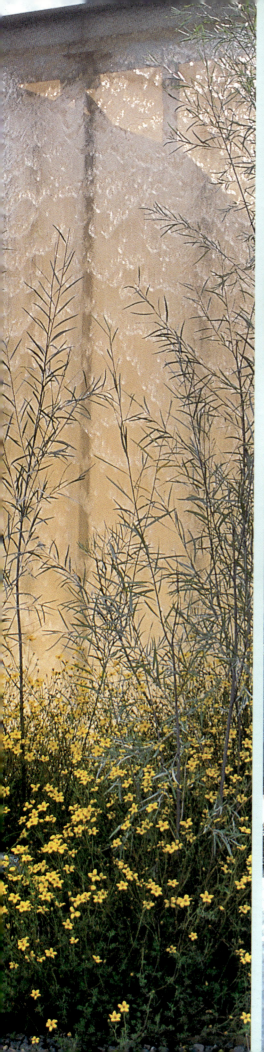

elements

For a well-designed garden to have style and character, honest purpose and sensitive creativity are required. All the elements need to have a harmonious balance of form and function with an aesthetic and decorative appeal. A well-designed and perfectly constructed water feature can make more impact on a garden than any other addition, and the ornamental elements need to relate to and enhance its appearance.

A romantic garden with countryside flowers and a gurgling stream, for example, may benefit from a tiny rustic wooden bridge or one made from strategically placed slabs of natural stone, whereas the ideal crossing for a formal and contemporary pool may be asymmetrical concrete blocks set on piers or a sheet of shiny perforated metal. Wooden decking is a natural companion to water and can be combined with pebbles and pea shingle to create decorative elements for a seashore or rooftop garden.

**above** In this design, a single stone slab bridges the formal canal with the interconnecting levels of wooden decking above, and tufts of green grasses sprout up among the pebbles like tiny green fountains.

**right** This contemporary garden demonstrates how water, stone and plants may be combined together while still retaining their individual characteristics.

# bridges

The bridge is the most important architectural feature to be developed in conjunction with water. Apart from its utilitarian purpose, a bridge has great symbolic significance in both Chinese and Japanese gardens.

A bridge is, in essence, a path to cross water. It may be an extrovert structural feature in its own right or a seamless link and subtle continuation of a path or walkway. It may be raised in a graceful arch to create a viewing point across a pool or consist of no more than a simple flat slab bisecting a formal canal where the water laps at your feet. The materials and design depend largely on the style of the garden and water feature, and there are innumerable historical references from which to seek inspiration.

The ancient Chinese Taoist religion believed that everything in nature had its own spirit, and the gardens its followers created were scaled-down reflections of the natural landscape. Rocks and water were essential symbolic objects, and the interconnecting bridges, often constructed from wood or long flat stones, were designed to replicate the natural landscape. The bridges not only provided access across the water but also created platforms from which to contemplate the reflections of passing clouds in the sky.

**above** The simple curve of a traditional stone bridge perfectly complements the rural setting of a gently running stream, and its muted colour blends with the bark of the surrounding trees.

**left** In a contemporary urban garden with its formal lines, simple styling and natural materials, a simple slab is all that is required to cross a stone and deck-edged canal.

The moon bridge, with its central arch whose reflection completes the circle in the water, was adopted by the Japanese when gardening was introduced from China in the 7th century. In 12th-century Japan, the Zen Buddhist priests, following their philosophy of austerity, humility and simplicity, created meditative gardens where the rhythm and movement between water features, planting and walkways has inspired many contemporary landscape designers.

The English Landscape Movement of the 18th century, associated most famously with the designs of Lancelot "Capability" Brown (1716–83), achieved harmony by contriving to recreate nature as faithfully as possible and on a major scale. Bridges were often the only architectural feature, usually made of simple stone and with three or five arches, often decorated with balustraded rails, statues or urns. These bridges were sometimes positioned at the end of a stretch of water to give the impression that it continued further. For today's gardener, traditional painted wooden bridges, with detailing from Gothic to "Chinese Chippendale", may be adapted to suit gardens of all sizes.

**above left** One of the mainstays of the English Landscape Movement was the bridge. Later versions included this "Chinese Chippendale" design.

**above right** The simplest of wooden bridges crosses the gently moving streams and lagoons in the water gardens at Longstock, Hampshire, in England.

# *case study* bridge garden

Water is used in a number of different ways in this Dutch garden. As well as the canal, which runs the length of the garden, there is also a pool area and a greenhouse over which water gently trickles.

This example of a modern Dutch garden breaks with tradition with its enclosed urban space behind a house and office. The result is an utterly contemporary and innovative garden that combines the formality of traditional Dutch design with a distinctive and witty modern twist.

A small 13 x 8m (42 x 26ft) space has been transformed into a capacious outside room that is both eminently functional and easy to maintain. To create its delightfully light and playful appearance, the designer experimented with the effects and impact of water, the application of strong colours and materials, and the dramatic use of diagonal shapes to visually increase the perception of space.

The use of running water is the most important feature in the garden. Its source is a perforated pipe fitted on top of the glass-roofed greenhouse, from where the water sprinkles down in a gentle cascade to drip like heavy rainfall into an asymmetrically shaped pool below. From here, the water is circulated in underground pipes back to its source. Adjoining the pool is a long, concrete-lined canal. The canal divides a raised deck, which provides a sheltered sun spot for containerized broad-leaved *Catalpa*, from a gravelled dining space. The two areas are linked by a textured-metal bridge and steps.

The view of the garden from the inside has been considered with meticulous care. From the bedroom balcony there is a strong impression of asymmetrical shapes and textures, and from the office window there is the restful sight of water softly trickling over the glass roof. The exterior wall colours make the most of shadow effects.

**below** Looking out from an office and across a gravelled courtyard can be seen a greenhouse where water sprinkles down the glass roof.

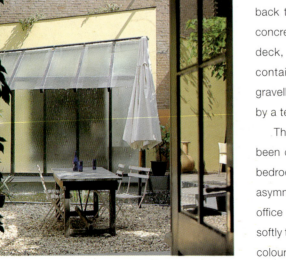

**above** From the roof, the water drips into a formal pond linked to a long canal, illuminated at night with a series of wall-mounted downlighters.

**right** The application of strong colours and materials is clearly seen from above, and shows how the canal is crossed by a diagonal, textured-metal bridge.

# islands and stepping stones

**above** Large and irregular stone slabs appear to float across this pond. The stones link the curved granite setts on the terrace to a narrow deck promontory on the opposite side.

**left** This floating garden combines fixed tiers of container-grown plants with rafts of floating plants. The floating plants drift across the water in between the circular wood-decked pontoons, which create solid wooden steps to the seating area at the back of the pool.

There is something intrinsically romantic about stepping stones across water. A series of such stones can create an inviting path across a small pool or tiny stream.

Like any other permanent element, stepping stones need to be designed in harmony with the style and character of the water feature they are crossing. Whereas a bridge may stand as an architectural feature in its own right, stepping stones are best designed as a seamless continuation of a path that leads to the water's edge and over the water on the same level.

In formal settings this path may be a straight line of concrete blocks or bricks set on sturdy piers spaced apart to create a safe and comfortable distance between each step. Slabs with a textured surface provide a better grip and these need to overhang the supporting piers, which may be camouflaged by being painted black. This creates the illusion that the stepping stones appear to be floating in the water. These piers may also be constructed in such a manner as to allow small gaps in the brickwork for fish and other aquatic creatures to seek sanctuary, particularly in a formal pond where the perimeter has straight sides and there is little planting.

If space permits, it may be possible to design steps across the water, emulating the shape of giant lily pads. These may be constructed from wood and elevated just above the water level by means of sturdy concrete piers. Creating a series of tiny individual islands offers attractive possibilities: sitting in the middle of the pool and dangling your feet in the cool water, or observing the aquatic life more closely. For really large-scale pools, the stepping stones could create a pathway across the water to a fabricated or natural island, which can be made into the ultimate hideaway and the most secluded part of a garden.

**below** The juxtaposition of crisp walkways of softly weathered decking with huge granite slabs create a harmonious effect in this tranquil water garden.

# water and sculpture

Water may emerge from a carved mascaron or spill over a

hand-beaten metal bowl, but the rise and fall of sprays and

cascades can create the most exciting sculptural effects.

**above** A sophisticated pump provides the technology to activate a constant stream of bubbles in this sculpture.

Garden design can so often be taken far too seriously, resulting in a space that is beautifully manicured, horticulturally sound and aesthetically correct but at best rather staid and at worse, boring. The element of water offers scores of opportunities to add movement and excitement and even sheer fun. Many of the popes and princes who created gardens during the Renaissance liked nothing better than playing jokes on unsuspecting visitors who were soaked by a jet or spray of water that suddenly appeared from a wall by the side of a path or next to the seat of a bench. The Italian phrase *giochi d'acqua*, literally meaning "water games", encapsulates the concept of having fun with water.

Henry VIII, renowned for his hearty sense of humour, installed surprise fountains at his palaces at Hampton Court, Nonsuch and Whitehall, and in the garden created by the sixth Duke of Devonshire at Chatsworth a tiny metal tree sprinkles tiny drops of rain from the tips of its leaves. Over the centuries, the concept of playful water has been virtually lost, with the exception of the scores of poorly executed and cheap statuary that squirt water from various appendages. With electronic and digitally programmed pumps, the elements of surprise and delight are now being used by water designers to enhance the sculptural effect of moving water. Fabulous effects can be created by fibre-optic lighting or the installation of a vapour machine.

On a smaller and less costly scale, a collection of hand-picked rounded stones surrounding a small fountain makes a simple and pleasing natural sculpture, and can be constantly rearranged to create different movements and sound patterns.

**right** Sculpture in the water garden does not have to be on a grand scale or involve the complexities of installing moving water, as is shown by this collection of coloured-glass spheres in a small pond. The surrounding foliage blends with the spheres to create a pleasing effect.

**right** In the centre of a garden designed for quiet contemplation is a hand-beaten metal bowl, overflowing into a rolled steel pool. The moving water creates a soft and pleasing sound while maintaining a reflective surface to catch the changing movements of the clouds.

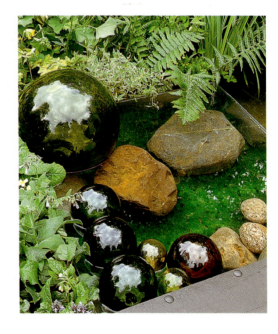

# *case study* silver water sculpture

The dramatic silver sculpture in the centre of the circular pool is the

focus of this contemporary garden, which has been designed to act

as an outdoor living space for relaxing, dining and entertaining.

**left** The sound of tumbling water is heard around the garden as it falls in a broad cascade into the still pool below. The planting scheme is based on architectural plants, a theme which is in keeping with the bold lines and modern sculpture in the rest of the garden.

Creating an inviting space in which to relax and unwind is many people's dream when designing a garden. The main aim behind this courtyard-style garden is the creation of a quiet retreat in which to escape the strains of modern life, soothed by the calming effects of water.

The smooth, clean lines of the gently curving decking area and the circular pool, as well as the pale colours of the hard landscaping, help to give this ultra-modern garden a soothing, tranquil atmosphere. The large circular pool, with steps leading up to the wooden decking area, is the focal point of the garden. This pool is enhanced by a shiny, funnel-shaped sculpture, which breaks the surface of the still, clear water and reflects the colours of the sky. The effect is of a miniature whirlpool spiralling down into the depths below.

The gentle ripples of the pool are disturbed only by a broad sheet of cascading water. The sound of the water is audible all around the decking, making the space a peaceful and mesmerizing place in which to sit. The cascade is fed by a stepped rill, which is narrower than the cascade, but falls into a reservoir beneath the decking where it is collected before falling into the pool. At the top of the rill is a water feature, above which stands a circular sculpture, thus continuing the prodominant theme of gentle circles and relaxing curves.

**above** The pool can be reached by a short flight of steps. The edge of the pool is just large enough to accommodate a comfortable chair, while the muted colours of the pool surround and the raised decking area are conducive to relaxation and quite contemplation.

**left** The shimmering effect of the highly polished, funnel-shaped water sculpture is in keeping with the contemporary materials used throughout the garden.

## *project* water cubes

The hollow cement blocks used in the construction industry for building foundations provide the basic structure for creating a very simple and flexible water feature. The cavities in one of the bricks are filled with water, while the other bricks are left dry.

Different configurations of these bricks, either laid flat or on their ends, are a practical solution for introducing water in an outside place where excavation is impossible. The industrial nature of the materials also makes this design appropriate for contemporary and urban surroundings.

**left** The tiny fountains contrast with the dull concrete. They sparkle with the aid of the aquatic lights and the reflection against the cube interiors.

**right** The cubes can be arranged in a number of ways to create a variety of visual effects.

**below** Tender dwarf bamboo is very effective planted *en masse* in strong-shaped containers.

### You will need

| | | |
|---|---|---|
| Hollow cement bricks (foundation blocks) | Acrylic or chrome enamel paint in silver or ultramarine blue | 2 small pumps |
| Plastic sheet | | 2 aqua lights |
| Petroleum jelly | Water-based silver paint | Copper pipe |
| Cement repair mix | Electric drill with 6mm (¼in) and 12mm (½in) drill bits | Felt-tipped pen |
| Selection of paintbrushes, including 2 small artist's brushes | | Pipe cutters |
| | Waterproof varnish | Electricity supply (circuit breaker) |
| White primer (for cement, plaster) | Silicone sealant | Miniature bamboos and cobbles for decoration |
| | Screwdriver | |

**2** Paint the inside of all the other bricks with white primer. Take care to paint neat edges with the artist's brush. Prime the brick that is to hold water once the cement has dried.

**1** To fill in the base of the brick that is to contain the water, dampen the inside of the cavities where the cement will adhere to the brick. Lay out a piece of plastic sheet, large enough for one brick. Coat the base of the brick with a thin layer of petroleum jelly. Place the brick front side up on the sheet. Following the manufacturer's instructions for the cement repair mix, fill the bottom of both cavities to a depth of about 4cm (1½in). Ensure the cement is level and has made good contact with the sides of the brick. Any holes might cause leaks. Leave to dry.

**3** Once dry, paint over the primer in the bricks that are to remain dry with your chosen acrylic or chrome enamel paint. The brick that is to hold the water should only be painted with a water-based paint because it will be sealed with a varnish that will dissolve other paints.

**4** (left) Drill holes for the cabling for the lights and pumps. Each cavity needs two holes: a 6mm (¼in) hole for the pump cable and a 12mm (½in) hole for the aqua-light cable. Lay the brick so that the side is facing up. Drill the holes about 4cm (1½in) above the cement layer (i.e. 6cm/2½in from the bottom). The holes should come well within the width of the cavity. Mark each hole with a pen, then drill all four holes until you have two 6mm (¼in) holes and two 12mm (½in) holes.

**5** Clean the dust out of the cavities in the water brick. Seal the cavities with the waterproof varnish. Leave to set.

**6** Remove the electrical plugs from the pump cables. Feed the cable of each pump through the 6mm (¼in) holes from the inside of the cavities. Pull the cable out on the other side so that you have a few inches of slack. Replace the plugs. To fit the lights, carefully remove the glass sheaths and the bulbs. Make sure you do not touch the halogen bulb with bare fingers. Push the light cables through the 12mm (½in) holes from the outside so that it is inside the cavity. Replace the bulbs and sheaths.

**7** Seal in the cables so that the water brick will be watertight. Using the silicone sealant, squeeze into and around the holes and cables, both on the inside and the outside of the cavities, ensuring that there are no gaps at all. You may need to apply the sealant in two or three stages, allowing it to set between each stage. Leave undisturbed for 24 hours.

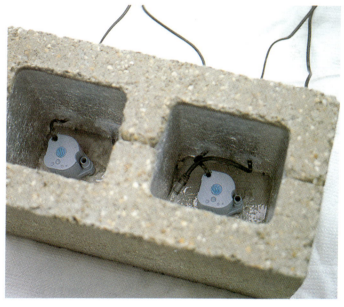

**8** Place a copper pipe, which has been painted with chrome paint, over the pump outlet. Mark the level for cutting the pipe down to size with a felt-tipped pen. Cut down the pipe to the correct height with pipe cutters (*see inset*).

**9** The dry bricks and the water brick can be arranged in any number of configurations. When you are happy with the design, fill the water brick with water, plug in the pumps and lights and test the flow of water. Consult a qualified electrician if you are installing any kind of electrical equipment with a water feature.

## You will need

19mm (¾in) copper pipe

Polystyrene (plastic foam) sphere

PVA (white) glue

Copper sheet

Metal cutters

Quick-drying waterproof tile adhesive and spoon

Junior hacksaw

Fibreglass bowl

Submersible pump, 4 litres (1 gallon) per minute

Electric drill

Silicone sealant

Metal punchings

Electricity supply (circuit breaker)

## *project* copper sphere

This small water feature is portable and can be used indoors as well as outdoors for the enjoyment of the soothing sound of the trickling water. Its diminutive size means it can be used as a table feature or alternatively it could be mounted on a plinth of some kind to create a more prominent feature in the garden.

The copper is shiny at first and naturally catches the light as the water flows over its surface. Over time, the copper will dull and turn green, which adds to its charm. However, if you would like to retain the original shine, then a clear lacquer can be added at any stage of the natural aging process.

**left and right** Illuminate this feature on a summer's evening with orange candles.

**below** Recycled clear glass or scrap metal makes a shiny base for the copper sphere.

**1** (*left*) Using the copper pipe, push out a hole in each half of the polystyrene sphere, making sure that the holes are exactly opposite each other. Stick the two halves of the sphere together using the PVA glue, and allow to set.

**2** (*right*) While the sphere is setting, prepare the copper sheet by cutting it into approximately 19mm (¾in) squares with the metal cutters.

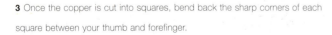

**3** Once the copper is cut into squares, bend back the sharp corners of each square between your thumb and forefinger.

**4** Mix a small quantity of the quick-drying tile adhesive at a time and spread over the polystyrene sphere using a spoon.

**5** (*left*) Starting at one of the holes, press the copper squares firmly into the tile adhesive. Work roughly around the sphere and overlap the squares as you go.

**6** (*right*) Cut the copper pipe to length so that it will pass through the sphere and into the bowl. Connect the pipe to the pump, then place the pipe and pump in the centre of the bowl. Drill a small hole in the side of the bowl at the bottom for the electric cable from the power supply to the pump. Seal the hole with a silicone sealant.

**7** Add the metal punchings, ensuring that the pipe remains upright. Add water to the bowl (*see inset*).

**8** Slide the polystyrene sphere over the copper pipe so that it rests on the metal punchings with the copper pipe flush with the top of the sphere.

# water and light

Light is the most important element when designing with

water – tiny droplets sparkle in bright sunshine and still pools

reflect all the colours and shapes surrounding them.

Bright sunlight on moving or still water has a magical quality, and light from an artificial source can quite easily replicate this effect. Even the tiniest fountain can include a small low-voltage halogen light with the bulb hidden from view so it creates the effect of a central core of pure white bubbling water. The key factor in combining artificial light with water is that the source should never be visible, nor any of the cables or equipment controlling it. As water and electricty can be a dangerous combination, it is wise to consult a reputable and qualified electrician for any installations.

Uplighters that can dramatize a cascade by night can be concealed by positioning them behind the waterfall or at the sides behind rocks, or by using discreet, black, non-reflective lampholders. Equally dramatic is a light source at the bottom of a pool exactly beneath the point where the cascade hits the water's surface. In formal pools and similarly in swimming pools, where the reservoir has a solid construction, submersible lights need to be recessed into the sides where they will be invisible during the day and the effect of shafts of light across the pool illuminate the bottom. For night-time bathing it is also judicious to consider lighting the perimeter of the pool with recessed lights so the edge is clearly visible. In natural ponds lighting can be concealed beneath clumps of plants or attached to the piers of stepping stones or under a bridge. Artificial lighting is always most effective when it illuminates an object but never directly the water.

**below** Lighting has been cleverly concealed beneath the rim of this black basin in order to illuminate the sheet of brimming water as it falls over the edge.

**right** This is a modern interpretation of a traditional Zen garden. It has a formal pool flanked by beds of raked gravel with strategically placed giant rocks. These rocks represent islands, and the gravel is the waves crashing into them. Recessed uplighters in the base of the pool and a machine creating a soft mist add a contemporary twist to an ancient theme.

# *project* illuminated tubes

This free-standing water sculpture is ideal for a small space, particularly if you are looking for an unusual feature with maximum impact.

The purpose of the feature is to bring some height and architectural form to a small courtyard or terrace and to complement any climbers or tall plants. It could even be situated in a conservatory (porch).

An adaptation of a Japanese drainpipe, this sculpture makes an interesting feature during the day or night. The flow of the water is soothing to listen to and is determined by the size and length of the chain. This disrupts the movement of the water sufficiently to create a soft sound. The water also sparkles gently in the sun or in a spotlight.

The tubes, which are coloured blue on the inside, and the sparkling movement of the water are the fine details that complete this contemporary water feature.

**left and above** The industrial effect of this unusual water sculpture is provided by the materials that have been used, including metal tubing, nuts and bolts, and a chain.

**far left** Similar galvanized tubing may be cut to size to provide "sleeves" for less attractive containers. A mulch of recycled glass "gravel" glitters and glistens when caught with a fine spray of water.

## You will need

| | |
|---|---|
| 1.5m (5ft) galvanized tubing | 24 nuts and washers |
| Electric angle grinder | 6 large bolts, 20cm (8in) in length |
| Metal file | Waterproof electrical glands |
| Metal rule and pencil | Small pump |
| 1.8m (6ft) timber, 30cm (12in) by 1cm (½in) | Submersible light |
| Electric drill, plus an 18mm (¹¹⁄₁₆in) and 22mm (¹³⁄₁₆in) drill bit | Plastic hose, 22mm (¹³⁄₁₆in) in diameter |
| Wood stain or paint | Spanner |
| Paintbrush | 22–15mm (¹³⁄₁₆–⁹⁄₁₆in) copper reducer |
| Hacksaw | 19mm (¾in) stainless steel nail |
| 2.4m (8ft) copper pipe, 22mm (¹³⁄₁₆in) in diameter | 1.8m (6ft) stainless steel chain |
| 4 right-angle copper bends | Piece of black foam, 2.5cm (1in) thick |
| Concrete mix | Electricity supply (circuit breaker) |
| Masking tape | |
| Metal spray paint | |

**1** Mark and cut the length of tubing into five or six pieces using the angle grinder. You will need a 900mm (36in) piece for the base tube, a 300mm (12in) piece for the top tube and four of any size for the tubes in between. File off any sharp splinters.

**2** Mark out a centre line and the spacings for the bolts and copper pipes on the length of wood. Drill the holes for the bolts with the 18mm (¹¹⁄₁₆in) drill bit. Drill a 22mm (¹³⁄₁₆in) hole at the top and bottom of the wood for the copper pipes (*see inset*).

**3** Paint or stain the drilled piece of wood in a colour that will suit the design of your garden.

**4** Drill an 18mm (¹¹⁄₁₆in) hole for the bolts in the centre of each of the tubes apart from the base tube. For the base tube, drill an 18mm (¹¹⁄₁₆in) hole approximately 200mm (8in) from the top end and a 22mm (¹³⁄₁₆in) hole for the copper pipe about 100mm (4in) from the other end, ensuring that it aligns with the 22mm (¹³⁄₁₆in) hole that you drilled earlier in the piece of wood. Drill a 22mm (¹³⁄₁₆in) hole in the top tube about 50mm (2in) from the top, again in line with the hole in the wood. Drill two more 18mm (¹¹⁄₁₆in) holes in the base tube for the waterproof glands for the electric cables from the pump and the light.

**5** Cut two lengths of copper pipe, about 250mm (10in) long (*see inset*). Connect one of the lengths to a right-angle bend and insert into the 22mm (¹³⁄₁₆in) hole in the base tube with the angle inside the tube. Mix a small quantity of concrete. Lay the tube with the copper pipe on a level surface, then pour the concrete mix into the tube to a depth of about 200mm (8in), being careful not to get any concrete into the pipe.

**6** Wrap the cut tubes with masking tape at each end and spray paint inside each one.

**7** When dry, attach the tubes to the wood with the nuts, washers and bolts, leaving a space of 100mm (4in) between the wood and the tubes.

**8** Attach the waterproof electrical glands to the base tube and feed through the cables from the submersible pump and light. Attach approximately 600mm (24in) of the 22mm (¹³⁄₁₆in) hose to the pump and connect to the copper pipe in the base tube. Tighten the glands with a spanner to prevent leaks (*see inset*).

**9** Cut the remaining copper pipe so that it will fit between the two 22mm (¹³⁄₁₆in) holes in the wooden board. This will be approximately 1.8m (6ft). Attach the length of copper pipe to the bottom pipe with a right-angle bend. At the top of the board, attach the length of copper pipe to the other 250mm (10in) length of pipe, which passes through the wood and tubing holes, using another right-angle bend. Attach the fourth right-angle bend to the short length of pipe inside the tube.

**10** Drill a hole through both sides of the 15mm (⁹⁄₁₆in) end of the copper reducer, large enough for a 19mm (¾in) nail. Feed the nail through one side of the reducer, through one end of the chain, then through the second hole (*see inset*). Attach to the right-angle bend in the top tube.

**11** Place the connected pump in the lower tube. Cut a circle from the black foam so that it is slightly larger than the circumference of the metal tubes. Cut a cross in the middle of the foam that is large enough for the base of the light to be squeezed through.

**12** Fit the foam and light into the base tube. Fill the base tube with water and switch on the pump.

# *blueprint* making a wooden bridge

Even a small pool or stream can be enhanced by a simple bridge. Keep the structure in proportion to the width of the water and avoid having too steep an arch or too much superstructure if the bridge is only short in length. The illustration shows the construction of a simple wooden plank bridge, which uses decking planks secured at right angles to the supporting joists. The minimum width is 60cm (2ft) and the length should not exceed 2.5m (8ft) without an intermediate support.

**1** To provide a good foundation for the ends of the bridge, lay concrete blocks, measuring 1.2m x 20cm x 10cm (4ft x 8in x. 4in), on either side of the water. Position the blocks a minimum of 23cm (9in) from the water, so that the sloping pool sides do not affect their stability.

**2** Before the concrete sets, place the two supporting bridge bearers or joists 45cm (18in) apart, and hold right-angled brackets on their inside edge to mark the position of the bolts. Bed the bolts into the concrete with the screw end protruding by 2.5cm (1in). Bolt the brackets on to the concrete when dry.

**3** Screw the joists to the brackets when the concrete is thoroughly dry. Lay the decking planks over the bearers, 1cm (½in) apart, in order to allow for expansion when wet.

**4** Screw in the end planks first, then stretch a string between them to act as a guide for positioning the rest of the planks.

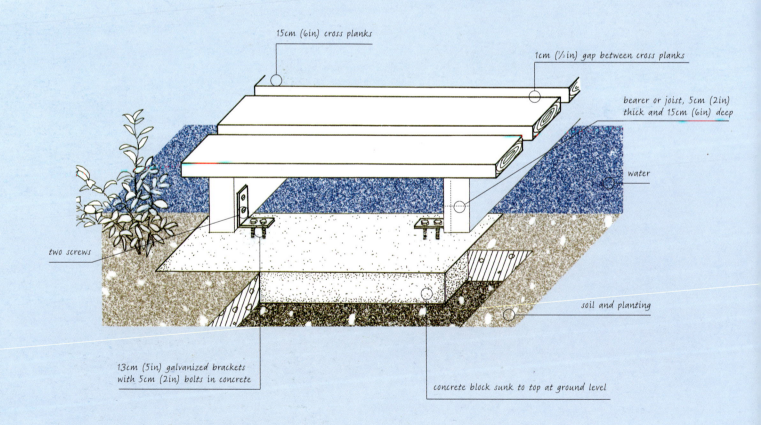

15cm (6in) cross planks

1cm (½in) gap between cross planks

bearer or joist, 5cm (2in) thick and 15cm (6in) deep

water

two screws

soil and planting

13cm (5in) galvanized brackets with 5cm (2in) bolts in concrete

concrete block sunk to top at ground level

# *blueprints* constructing islands

A wildlife pool is particularly suitable for a small island, which will act as a safe retreat for several small creatures. Although it is possible to build an island after the pond has been built, it is always advisable to consider the addition of an island during the pool-building process, rather than as an afterthought because the pool will need emptying in order to build on the lining. The diagrams below explain how to install a wet and dry island before the pond is constructed.

### WET ISLAND WITH MOUND MADE BEFORE POND CONSTRUCTION

**1** A wet island can be built before the pond is constructed by building up a mound of soil to within a few inches of the waterline. Create a mound of soil in the centre of the pool during the initial excavation.

**2** To hold the mound of soil in position, stack turves on top of each other all around the island so that the upper turf is just below the waterline. Lay the bottom turf directly on top of the flexible liner.

**3** Because the liner is below the level of the water, the mound of soil is kept moist. Plant up the island with a selection of moisture-loving plants, such as *Iris sibirica* (Siberian iris), primulas and astilbes.

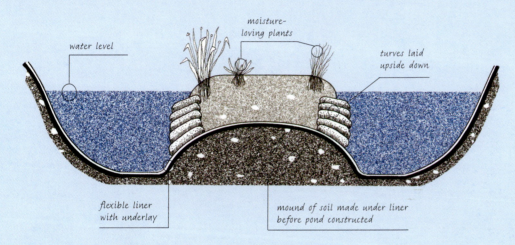

water level

moisture-loving plants

turves laid upside down

flexible liner with underlay

mound of soil made under liner before pond constructed

### DRY ISLAND WITH MOUND MADE BEFORE POND CONSTRUCTION

**1** If it is considered at the design stage, an island can be "dry". Create a large mound of soil in the centre of the pool during the initial excavation.

**2** Lay the underlay and flexible liner over the top of the soil mound. Cut a hole in the underlay and liner so that an area of soil is exposed. Ensure that the liner is taken well above the waterline.

**3** Add a further mound of soil on top of the foundation to create a gently curving island. Stack turves on top of each other all around the island to hold the dry soil in place.

**4** Because the liner is taken above the waterline, the mound of soil is kept dry.

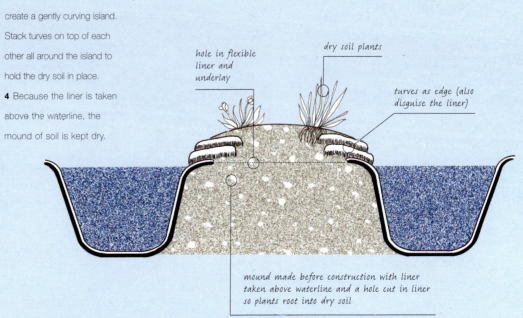

hole in flexible liner and underlay

dry soil plants

turves as edge (also disguise the liner)

mound made before construction with liner taken above waterline and a hole cut in liner so plants root into dry soil

# *blueprints* building stepping stones

Where a bridge may be too heavy or too formal a structure as a means of crossing the water, stepping stones make an excellent alternative for small pools. For formal situations a paving slab, which overhangs a supporting pier of bricks, makes an excellent stepping stone. The following instructions explain how to construct a formal stepping stone and require bricklaying skills to make the pier. For streams or informal pools, large flat-topped boulders are both functional and natural in appearance.

## FORMAL, USING A PAVING STONE

**1** As the site for each individual stepping stone will need to support the weight of a person as well as the brick pier, you will need to provide a concrete foundation. Before laying the underlay and flexible liner, identify the site for each stepping stone and lay a slab of concrete, 7.5–10cm (3–4in) thick and 60cm (2ft) square, on a bed of hardcore or rubble.

**2** Place the underlay and flexible liner over the foundations as soon as they have set firm.

**3** Mortar courses of brick on to the liner in order to form a square pier a few inches above the water line.

**4** Mortar a paving slab, which is larger than the pier, on to the top course of bricks and check levels with a spirit (carpenter's) level.

**5** Wait until the mortar hardens before filling the pool and using the stepping stones.

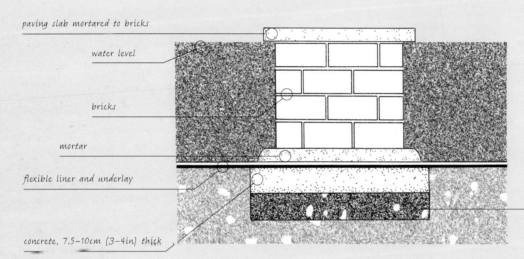

paving slab mortared to bricks

water level

bricks

mortar

flexible liner and underlay

concrete, 7.5–10cm (3–4in) thick

hardcore or rubble before liner laid

## INFORMAL, USING A LARGE BOULDER WITH A FLAT TOP

**1** To construct stepping stones using large boulders, you will need to ensure that the boulders have flattish tops in the interests of stability and safety.

**2** After laying the underlay and flexible liner during the excavation of the pool, work out the number and position of stepping stones you would like to include.

**3** Put a circular layer of mortar, 8–10cm (3–4in) thick, on top of the flexible liner, forming a concave shape in the mortar in order to give the boulder greater stability.

**4** Bed each of the boulders into a layer of mortar and allow to set thoroughly before filling the pool with water and walking on the stepping stones.

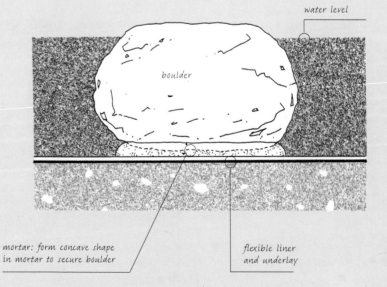

water level

boulder

mortar: form concave shape in mortar to secure boulder

flexible liner and underlay

# *blueprint* lighting and electrics

Garden lighting can be an exciting addition to a water feature. The fine spray of a fountain or the ripples of a waterfall caught in submerged light are just two of the many possibilities that will extend the impact of the water. Increasingly, for safety reasons, more lighting applications are being manufactured with low-voltage systems with a transformer in order to reduce the voltage. This illustration shows a low-voltage lighting application used to illuminate the main features of a water garden.

**1** Install a transformer suitable for indoors inside the house or garage.

**2** Lead the cable from the transformer through the frame of a window or through a wall.

**3** Where the cable crosses any heavily used part of the garden, it is prudent to thread the cable through a plastic conduit just under the ground to any of the following lighting applications.

**4** A low spotlight facing away from the windows is a simple but most effective way of highlighting a cobble fountain.

**5** The cable can easily be extended to floating or underwater lights to catch the spray of a fountain or the turbulence of a waterfall.

**6** If there is an ornament or specimen tree on the far side of the pool from the house, the feature, when lit from beneath, will be reflected on the surface of the water in the evening.

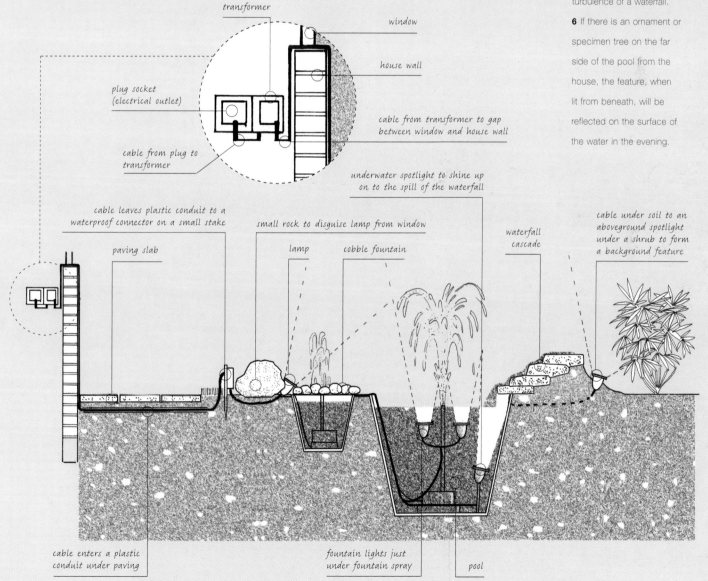

transformer

window

house wall

plug socket
(electrical outlet)

cable from transformer to gap
between window and house wall

cable from plug to
transformer

underwater spotlight to shine up
on to the spill of the waterfall

cable leaves plastic conduit to a
waterproof connector on a small stake

small rock to disguise lamp from window

waterfall
cascade

cable under soil to an
aboveground spotlight
under a shrub to form
a background feature

paving slab

lamp

cobble fountain

cable enters a plastic
conduit under paving

fountain lights just
under fountain spray

pool

Creating a successful water garden relies on a basic understanding of the differences between the plants that enjoy this specialized environment. Fully submerged aquatic plants are essential for inhibiting the growth of green water algae. Free-floating plants also help to maintain the water's clarity by shading the surface and depriving algae of necessary sunlight. The roots of marginal plants require immersion in water to thrive, and should not be confused with moisture-loving plants, which need a constantly damp soil that is never saturated.

## HARDINESS RATINGS

**Frost tender**  Plant tolerates temperatures down to 5°C (41°F).

**Half hardy**  Plant tolerates temperatures down to 0°C (32°F).

**Frost hardy**  Plant tolerates temperatures down to -5°C (23°F).

**Fully hardy**  Plant tolerates temperatures down to -15°C (5°F).

**right** *Nymphaea* 'Lucida' (right) is a hardy waterlily that tolerates partial shade. *Mentha cervina* (far top right) thrives in containers. The yellow-green *Hosta* 'Sum and Substance' (far bottom right) grows well in sun or partial shade.

key plants

# submerged aquatics and floating plants

This group includes those decorative aquatics that add variety to the surface of the water in the deeper part of the pond as well as a selection of submerged oxygenators and floating plants that are important, especially in new pools, in helping to reduce levels of algae.

*Aponogeton distachyos*

*Callitriche hermaphroditica*

### *Aponogeton distachyos* (water hawthorn, Cape pondweed)

This South African perennial has double spikes of vanilla-scented, white flowers with black anthers in spring and autumn.

**aspect** Full sun to partial shade.
**planting depth** 15–45cm (6–18in).
**spread** 1.2m (4ft).
**hardiness** Frost hardy.

### *Callitriche hermaphroditica* – syn. *C. autumnalis* (autumn starwort)

One of the few varieties of submerged oxygenating plants that is active in the winter months, this evergreen perennial provides an attractive home for spawning fish. The tiny, narrow, elongated, light green leaves, 50cm (20in) long, are almost completely submerged.

**aspect** Full sun or partial shade.
**planting depth** Up to 45cm (18in).
**spread** Indefinite.
**hardiness** Fully hardy.

### *Eleocharis acicularis* (spike rush)

This submerged, evergreen oxygenating perennial is widespread throughout Europe and North America. The dense, grassy tufts resemble an underwater lawn. It will produce spires of tiny, white flowers.

**aspect** Full sun to partial shade.
**planting depth** Up to 45cm (18in).
**spread** 60cm (2ft).
**hardiness** Fully hardy.

### *Hippuris vulgaris* (mare's tail)

The pale green, brush-like foliage of this oxygenator is ideal for ponds, slow-flowing streams and rivers. It can be extremely invasive if it is planted in clay-bottomed ponds.

**aspect** Full sun to partial shade.
**planting depth** 5–30cm (2–12in).
**spread** Indefinite.
**hardiness** Fully hardy.

### *Hottonia palustris* (water violet)

Although this deciduous perennial, which is native to Britain, will root in basal mud, it thrives best in deeper water where, in early summer, it thrusts up a mass of red-green stalks. These are divided at the ends with feathery, pale lavender or almost white flowers, which are held some 30–40cm (12–16in) above the water and the bright green, submerged leaves.

**aspect** Full sun to light shade.
**planting depth** 15–60cm (6–24in).
**spread** Indefinite.
**hardiness** Fully hardy.

### *Hydrocharis morsus-ranae* (frogbit)

Native to Europe, this floating perennial has horizontal stolons, which form new plants at the tips, and rosettes of rounded, glossy, mid-green leaves. In summer, bowl-shaped, three-petalled, white flowers, with a yellow spot at the base, rise above the surface of the water. Frogbit dies back in winter.

**aspect** Full sun to very light shade.
**planting depth** Up to 30cm (1ft).
**spread** Indefinite.
**hardiness** Fully hardy.

### *MYRIOPHYLLUM*

The 40 species of submerged aquatics in this genus are mainly from the southern hemisphere. The submerged stems are often long, bearing finely divided, almost feathery leaves, which are extremely attractive. The milfoils show a great diversity of habit, and many love to creep out of the water and scramble on to the surrounds of the pool.

*Hippuris vulgaris*

*Hydrocharis morsus-ranae*

*Myriophyllum aquaticum* – syn.
*M. brasiliense; M. proserpinacoides*
**(diamond milfoil, parrot's feather)**
This species is slightly tender and must be well
submerged in temperate climates if it is to survive the
winter. It is, nevertheless, extensively used in outdoor
pools, where the graceful foliage and stems take root
in the wet soil above the waterline.
**aspect** Full sun.
**planting depth** 10–60cm (4–24in).
**spread** Indefinite.
**hardiness** Frost hardy.

*Myriophyllum spicatum* **(spiked
water milfoil)**
The feathery appearance of this evergreen
oxygenator is created by whorls of four leaves, which
are very coarsely subdivided, along each stem.
The stems may be submerged or held just above the
surface of the water. In summer, minute pink or
yellow flowers appear in long spikes above the
surface of the water. It thrives best in alkaline water.
**aspect** Full sun to light shade.
**planting depth** 10–60cm (4–24in).
**spread** Indefinite.
**hardiness** Fully hardy.

*Nuphar lutea* **(brandy bottle lily,
spatterdock, yellow pond lily)**
This lesser-known member of the waterlily family
is a native European, deciduous species that is
very common in the wild. It is large and invasive,
and best suited to deep lakes rather than small
ponds. In summer, small yellow flowers appear
above the surface of the water.
**aspect** Full sun to moderate shade.
**planting depth** 1.2–5m (4–16ft).
**spread** Up to 1.8m (6ft).
**hardiness** Fully hardy.

*Pistia stratiotes* **(shell flower, water lettuce)**
An evergreen, floating perennial with pale green,
spreading and semi-upright, loose rosettes of
leaves with the texture of finely folded velvet,
this is considered an invasive nuisance in both
the USA and Africa. Being frost tender, however,
it is unlikely to cause problems in Europe. It can
be grown as an annual or overwintered indoors.
**aspect** Full sun.
**planting depth** 10–45cm (4–18in).
**spread** 30cm (1ft).
**hardiness** Frost tender.

*Pistia stratiotes*

*Ranunculus aquatilis* **(water buttercup,
water crowfoot)**
Although an excellent oxygenator for ponds, this
deciduous perennial requires periodic thinning in
order to prevent total invasion. It has dark green,
almost circular, floating leaves as well as very
finely divided and grass-like, submerged leaves
and buttercup-like, but pure white, golden-
centred flowers that float just above the surface.
**aspect** Full sun to moderate shade.
**planting depth** 10–60cm (4–24in).
**spread** Indefinite.
**hardiness** Fully hardy.

*Salvinia natans* **(water fern)**
Native to Central and South America, Africa and
India, this beautiful, free-floating fern bears soft,
silky-haired leaves, which are held in irregular
whorls of three leaves, two floating and one

*Salvinia natans*

*Ranunculus aquatilis*

submerged. Like *Pistia stratiotes*, it is frost tender,
but a small portion may be overwintered indoors.
**aspect** Full sun.
**planting depth** 10–45cm (4–18in).
**spread** Indefinite.
**hardiness** Frost tender.

*Stratiotes aloides* **(water soldier, water aloe)**
This is an intriguing semi-evergreen plant that looks
like a floating pineapple-top, with stiff, dark olive-
green, toothed leaves, which are arranged in loose
rosettes. In winter, when the leaves often die back,
the plant remains at the bottom of the pond where it
provides a valuable carpet of oxygenating foliage. In
mid-summer, it produces white or pink flowers.
**aspect** Full sun or very light shade.
**planting depth** 30–90cm (1–3ft).
**spread** 60cm (2ft).
**hardiness** Fully hardy.

*Stratiotes aloides*

Nymphaea 'Darwin'

## focus on waterlilies

These submerged aquatic plants, whose botanical name is *Nymphaea*, can be divided into two main groups: hardies and tropicals. All the hardy types will succeed without protection in temperate regions outdoors; the tropical plants, on the other hand, will need to be grown in a sunny glasshouse in all but the most favoured locations. The flowers vary in size, but they are generally always in proportion to the leaf, ranging from 2.5cm (1in) across in the pygmy varieties, to 30cm (1ft) across in some of the tropicals. There are waterlilies suitable for every size of pond, from barrels and tubs to extensive pools. All should be given a sunny, sheltered position without any water turbulence on their leaves. The planting depths given here refer to the depth of water above the crown or growing point and not to the depth of pond. The spread refers to the average area that the leaves will eventually cover, although in small planting containers they may not achieve these sizes. This selection includes species and cultivars that should be commercially available, although the tropical types are less easy to source in temperate areas.

Nymphaea 'Albert Greenberg'

Nymphaea 'Joey Tomocik'

### Nymphaea 'Albert Greenberg'

One of the most popular "sunset" tropicals, with its distinctive cup-like flowers, freedom of bloom and rich colour. The highly fragrant flowers are 15–18cm (6–7in) across, with yellow petals and orange tips, giving it an overall orange appearance.
**aspect** Full sun.
**planting depth** 30–38cm (12–15in).
**spread** 1.5–2.5m (5–8ft).
**hardiness** Tropical.

### Nymphaea 'Darwin'

The huge, double peony-style flowers of this waterlily measure 15–19cm (6–7½in) across. The inner petals are light pink, fading to a very light pink – almost white – outer petals surrounding pinkish yellow stamens. The new leaves are brownish, turning green as they mature.
**aspect** Full sun.
**planting depth** 30–60cm (1–2ft).
**spread** 1.2–1.5m (4–5ft).
**hardiness** Fully hardy.

### Nymphaea 'Joey Tomocik'

This outstanding cultivar has perfectly formed, very fragrant, deep yellow blooms held above the water.
**aspect** Full sun.
**planting depth** 30–38cm (12–15in).
**spread** 1.5–2.1m (5–7ft).
**hardiness** Tropical.

Nymphaea 'Madame Wilfon Gonnère'

### Nymphaea 'Leopardess'

A day-blooming cultivar with cup-like flowers, 10–13 cm (4–5in) across, which are clear blue with purple-tipped petals and yellow stamens. The nearly round, green-blotched purple leaves are 25–30cm (10–12in) across.
**aspect** Full sun.
**planting depth** 38–45cm (15–18in).
**spread** 1.2–1.5m (4–5ft).
**hardiness** Tropical.

### Nymphaea 'Madame Wilfon Gonnère'

The leaves of this aquatic perennial are mid-green, with overlapping lobes, and grow to 23–25cm (9–10in) in diameter. The young leaves are slightly bronze. The striking peony-shaped flowers, which reach 12cm (5in) across, are pink with pale pink outer petals and golden stamens.

**aspect** Full sun.

**planting depth** 38–45cm (15–18in).

**spread** 1.2m (4ft).

**hardiness** Fully hardy.

### Nymphaea 'Virginalis'

This aquatic perennial has rounded, pale green leaves, 22cm (9in) across. The large, white star-shaped flowers are fragrant, and have yellow stamens.

**aspect** Full sun.

**planting depth** 30–45cm (12–18in).

**spread** 0.9–1.2m (3–4ft).

**hardiness** Fully hardy.

*Nymphaea* 'Virginalis'

*Nymphaea* 'Leopardess'

*Nelumbo* leaves and "pepper pot" seed-head

## focus on lotus

The genus *Nelumbo* contains two species of rhizomatous marginals from Asia, north Australia and eastern North America, where they are found in the shallow margins or muddy banks of pools. They have circular leaves, held horizontally well above the water. The solitary flowers are borne on long stalks, and develop "pepper pot" seed-heads.

Lotus need ample sunshine or a high light intensity to ripen the thick roots in the mud. They need a minimum winter temperature of 5°C (41°F), but they will only do their best with a summer temperature of around 20°C (68°F). They should be grown in a large container of rich loam, with at least 30cm (12in) of soil under a covering of 8–15cm (3–6in) of water.

### Nelumbo lutea

This lotus has radial, concave-circular bluish green leaves, 50cm (20in) across and rose-like yellow flowers in summer.

**aspect** Full sun.

**height** 2m (6ft); **spread** Indefinite.

**hardiness** Frost tender.

### Nelumbo nucifera

The leaves of this lotus have wavy margins. The flowers are peony-like, and pink or white in colour.

**aspect** Full sun.

**height** 0.7–1.5m (28–60in); **spread** Indefinite.

**hardiness** Frost tender.

# marginal plants

The word "marginal" is used to describe water-garden plants that thrive with their roots and the basal part of their stem totally submerged in water or waterlogged soil. Marginals tolerate different depths of water, and it is important to check that plants that prefer shallow water are not planted too deep, even though in most cases short or seasonal changes in level will be tolerated. Deciduous marginals tolerate more water over their crowns in winter than in summer. Slightly deeper levels of water in the winter will also help to protect certain plants from frost and chilling winds.

Because so many marginals are vigorous growers, it is best to plant them in aquatic containers. The planting depth given for the following marginals is the depth above the crown or growing point and not the actual depth of water.

### ACORUS

The genus consists of two species of rhizomatous perennial, one semi-evergreen and the other deciduous, which originate from eastern Asia and are now widespread throughout the northern hemisphere. The sword-shaped leaves, similar to those of iris, have a pleasant scent when bruised. They are easy to grow.

### Acorus calamus (sweet flag, myrtle flag)

This vigorous deciduous species is ideal for wildlife ponds and provides good cover for waterfowl. The flower is the conical spadix, which resembles a small, brown horn that emerges laterally just below the tip of a leaf.
**aspect** Full sun to partial shade.
**planting depth** 5–30cm (2–12in).
**height** 60–90cm (2–3ft); **spread** Indefinite.
**hardiness** Fully hardy.

### Acorus gramineus (Japanese rush, dwarf sweet flag)

Smaller than *A. calamus*, this semi-evergreen species forms circular, fan-shaped, grassy clumps of mid-green leaves and has tiny, crook-

*Acorus gramineus 'Variegatus'*

*Arundo donax*

like "flower" spikes. It is ideal for smaller ponds. *A. gramineus* 'Variegatus' is an excellent cultivar with striking, silver-white variegated leaves.
**aspect** Full sun to partial shade.
**planting depth** 5–8cm (2–3in).
**height** 8–35cm (3–14in); **spread** 10–15cm (4–6in).
**hardiness** Half hardy.

### ALISMA

The species in this genus are found mainly in the northern hemisphere, where they grow on the muddy edges of marshes and lakes. The abundant seeds provide valuable food for wildlife and, unlike most aquatic seeds, they remain viable for up to a year.

### Alisma lanceolatum (narrow-leaved water plantain)

This perennial has attractive sprays of purple-pink flowers from early summer to early autumn and blue-green, lance-shaped leaves. It is suitable for all ponds and streams.

*Alisma plantago-aquatica*

*Butomus umbellatus*

**aspect** Full sun to partial shade.
**planting depth** 5–20cm (2–8in).
**height** 50–70cm (20–28in); **spread** 23cm (9in).
**hardiness** Fully hardy.

### Alisma plantago-aquatica (water plantain)

This deciduous perennial species has rosettes of oval, grey-green, semi-upright, ribbed leaves. The tiny pink flowers appear from mid- to late summer on stalks that reach 60–90cm (2–3ft).
**aspect** Full sun.
**planting depth** To 15cm (6in).
**height** 60–75cm (24–30in); **spread** 45cm (18in).
**hardiness** Fully hardy.

### Arundo donax (giant reed, giant rush)

With its attractive, bamboo-like foliage and mid-green, glaucous leaves, which can grow up to 60cm (2ft) in length, this clump-forming, rhizomatous perennial thrives best in frost-free conditions and needs protection from strong winds. It is ideal for conservatory (greenhouse)

*Calla palustris*

*Caltha palustris*

*Canna* 'Roi Humbert'

*Canna* 'Durban'

basal leaves have toothed margins, while the waxy, yellow, buttercup-like flowers can appear early after a mild winter, but generally peak in mid-spring. It is easy to grow and maintain. *C. palustris* 'Flore Pleno' has double yellow flowers and often produces a second flush in summer, while *C. palustris* var. *alba* has a more compact habit and white flowers with a yellow centre.

**aspect** Full sun.
**planting depth** 0–5cm (0–2in).
**height** 15–30cm (6–12in); **spread** 45cm (18in).
**hardiness** Fully hardy.

### *Caltha palustris* var. *palustris* – syn. *C. laeta*, *C. polypetala* (giant marsh marigold)

Suitable only for larger ponds, this variety has large, yellow flowers on stems that can reach as high as 1m (3ft). The dark green leaves can grow to as much as 25–30cm (10–12in) across.

**aspect** Full sun.
**planting depth** 10–13cm (4–5in).
**height** 90cm (3ft); **spread** 75cm (30in).
**hardiness** Fully hardy.

### *Canna* (Indian shot plant)

This genus contains 50 species of rhizomatous perennial, which originate from moist forest margins and open areas in Asia and tropical North and South America. The brightly coloured flowers, which appear in summer, are very exotic-looking. In frost-prone areas, they should be grown in containers and overwintered in a conservatory or greenhouse. They should not be kept in water during the winter.

There are a number of stunning cultivars, including 'Black Knight' (bronze foliage and very deep red flowers); 'Durban' (exotic pink- and purple-striped leaves and rich orange flowers); 'Fireside' (a smaller variety with large leaves and extra-large, red flowers); 'Roi Humbert' (vivid purple leaves and orchid-like, bright red flowers); 'Pink Sunburst' (multicoloured leaves with clear pink flowers); 'Striata' (light green to yellow-green striped leaves with large orange flowers); 'Verdi' (bronze-veined leaves and large orange flowers); and 'Yellow Humbert' (a taller plant with mid-green leaves and buttercup-yellow flowers).

**aspect** Sheltered full sun.
**planting depth** 5cm (2in).
**height** 1.5–2.1m (5–7ft); **spread** 50cm (20in).
**hardiness** Half hardy to frost tender.

water gardens and as a dramatic houseplant. *Arundo donax* var. *versicolor* (syn. *A. donax* 'Variegata') is a half-hardy variety with white-striped leaves. It is smaller than the species, growing to 1.8m (6ft) in height and spreading to 60cm (2ft).

**aspect** Full sun.
**planting depth** 5cm (2in).
**height** 5m (15ft); **spread** 1.5m (5ft).
**hardiness** Half hardy.

### *Butomus umbellatus* (flowering rush)

A perennial found in Europe, western Asia and north Africa, the flowering rush has long, twisted, mid-green leaves that turn dark purple and then dark green as they extend. Spreading umbels of cup-shaped, fragrant, rose-pink flowers appear in late summer.

**aspect** Full sun.
**planting depth** 8–15cm (3–6in).
**height** To 1.5m (5ft); **spread** 45cm (18in).
**hardiness** Fully hardy.

### *Calla palustris* (bog arum)

This perennial has conspicuous, long, creeping surface roots, heart-shaped, glossy, mid-green leaves, which are firm and leathery, and white flowers that resemble arum lilies (*Zantedeschia aethiopica*).

**aspect** Full sun to encourage flowering and fruiting.
**planting depth** 5cm (2in).
**height** 25cm (10in); **spread** Indefinite, but usually no more than 30cm (1ft).
**hardiness** Fully hardy.

### CALTHA

This is a widespread and common genus containing ten species of temperate marginal plants, which are extremely popular in both decorative and wildlife ponds.

### *Caltha palustris* (kingcup, marsh marigold)

This very widespread perennial grows all over the temperate and colder regions of the northern hemisphere. The nearly round, heart-shaped,

## CAREX

Containing 1,500 or more species, most of which occur in bogs, damp woodland or at the water's edge, this vast genus is found all over the world. As a result, there is one for every climate and type of soil. Sedges are mainly cultivated for their variegated or colourful foliage.

### Carex elata 'Aurea' – syn. Carex stricta 'Bowles' Golden' (Bowles' golden sedge)

One of the most decorative of all sedges, this deciduous plant grows in dense tufts of bright green leaves and produces brown flower spikes in late spring, after which the leaves turn bright yellow.
**aspect** Sun or partial shade.
**planting depth** Up to 15cm (6in).
**height** 38–70cm (15–28in); **spread** 45cm (18in).
**hardiness** Fully hardy.

### Carex nigra

This very attractive species has dark leaves and tiny, almost black, flowers, which are followed by black fruits in early autumn.
**aspect** Full sun.
**planting depth** Up to 15cm (6in).
**height** 25–60cm (10–24in); **spread** 45cm (18in).
**hardiness** Fully hardy.

### Carex riparia (great pond sedge)

This coarse and very tough plant is only suitable for large wildlife ponds. It often forms dense masses of blue-green leaves, which support a further cluster of foliage and brownish flower spikes. *C. riparia* 'Variegata' has creamy white leaves, with a narrow, green margin, and black flower-heads. It is smaller than the species, reaching a height of approximately 1m (3ft).

*Carex nigra*

**aspect** Sun or partial shade.
**planting depth** 10–15cm (4–6in).
**height** 1.5m (5ft); **spread** 90–120cm (3–4ft).
**hardiness** Fully hardy.
**expert's tip** When grown in the path of slow-moving water, *C. riparia* 'Variegata' acts as a natural filter, removing excess nutrients.

### Colocasia esculenta – syn. C. antiquorum (coco-yam, dasheen, green taro)

The tuberous deciduous and semi-evergreen perennials in this genus originate from the swampy areas of tropical Asia where they are grown as a staple food. They make a bold architectural statement in warm areas outdoors or in frost-free conservatories (porches). Contact with the sap may irritate the skin. The long-stalked, arrow- to heart-shaped, leaf blades of *C. esculenta* resemble elephants' ears. The leaf stalks are 8–25cm (3–10in) long, while the leaf blade grows up to 90cm (3ft) tall. The small, white flower spathes rarely occur on cultivated plants. *C. esculenta* 'Imperial Taro' has dark green leaves with violet-black blotches; 'Black

*Carex riparia*

Magic' has showy purple and black leaves and stems; 'Green Taro' has green leaves; and 'Violet Stemmed Taro' has dark purple stems and green leaves.
**aspect** Full sun.
**planting depth** Up to 30cm (1ft).
**height** 1.2–1.8m (4–6ft); **spread** 50cm (20in).
**hardiness** Frost tender.

### Cotula coronopifolia (brass buttons, bachelor's buttons, golden buttons)

Originating from South Africa, this annual or short-lived, half-hardy perennial has creeping, hairless, succulent stems and strongly scented, toothed leaves. Masses of button-like, bright yellow flower-heads appear in summer. Although it dies down in winter, it regenerates in the following spring from the self-sown seed produced throughout the year.
**aspect** Full sun.
**planting depth** 8–10cm (3–4in).
**height** 15–30cm (6–12in); **spread** To 30cm (1ft).
**hardiness** Frost hardy.

## CYPERUS

Most of the plants in this genus of around 600 species are tropical perennials grown for their elegant foliage and unusual inflorescences, which resemble an umbrella that has lost its cover. A few are frost hardy but in frost-prone areas, cyperus are grown as houseplants in a temperate greenhouse or conservatory.

### Cyperus involucratus – syn. C. alternifolius (umbrella grass)

This distinctive African perennial makes an excellent marginal in warm, sheltered pools in subtropical gardens. Its erect stems are topped

*Colocasia esculenta*

*Cyperus involucratus*

*Equisetum hyemale*

*Eriophorum angustifolium*

with several dark, radiating leaves. The tiny, yellow flowers, which appear in summer, turn brown after pollination.

**aspect** Full sun or partial shade.
**planting depth** 8–10cm (3–4in).
**height and spread** 60–75cm (24–30in).
**hardiness** Frost tender.

### *Cyperus longus* (galingale)

One of the only hardy members of the genus, this species can quickly colonize the muddy edges of lakes and rivers. For this reason, it should be grown in containers in small ponds. The brown spikelets of flowers appear from late spring to mid-summer.

**aspect** Full sun or partial shade.
**planting depth** 0–5cm (0–2in).
**height** 60–120cm (2–4ft); **spread** Indefinite.
**hardiness** Fully hardy.

### *Cyperus papyrus* (Egyptian paper rush)

In a very sheltered, tropical position or in a conservatory (porch) in temperate areas, this plant grows into a tall and very elegant specimen with mop-head tufts of fine, long, pendulous leaves and spikelets of brown flowers.

**aspect** Full sun.
**planting depth** 8–10cm (3–4in).
**height** 3.6–4.5m (12–15ft); **spread** 60–120cm (2–4ft).
**hardiness** Frost tender.

### *EQUISETUM*

The species in this very ancient genus, whose fossilized remains produce coal, are exceptionally invasive and occur in wet places in most regions of the world. They are best grown in a container.

### *Equisetum hyemale* (scouring rush)

The new shoots of this evergreen perennial, which has ridged, hollow, leafless stems, appear in spring and are particularly attractive. The stems contain silica and for years were used to polish metal; hence the common name.

**aspect** Sun or partial shade.
**planting depth** Up to 20cm (8in).
**height** 1.2m (4ft); **spread** Indefinite.
**hardiness** Fully hardy.

### *Equisetum scirpoides*

This species, which is smaller than *E. hyemale*, has finer, multi-branched, soft stems and is an ideal plant for container water gardens.

**aspect** Sun or partial shade.
**planting depth** Up to 5cm (2in).
**height** 15cm (6in); **spread** Indefinite.
**hardiness** Fully hardy.

### *Eriophorum angustifolium*

Found in bogs, where it spreads rapidly in the acid conditions, this marginal plant produces rather dull clumps of tough, needle-like leaves

and pretty, white, fluffy, pendent spikelets of flowers.

**aspect** Full sun.
**planting depth** 0–5cm (0–2in).
**height** 30cm (1ft); **spread** Indefinite.
**hardiness** Fully hardy.

### *Glyceria maxima* var. *variegata* – syn. *G. spectabilis* 'Variegata' (manna grass, sweet grass)

A highly ornamental and easy-to-grow perennial, this is a must-have plant for small ponds, providing it is grown in a container. It has cream-, white- and green-striped leaves, and in spring the young leaves are flushed with pink. The flowers form greenish spikelets in summer.

**aspect** Sun or partial shade.
**planting depth** 5–15cm (2–6in).
**height** 60cm (2ft); **spread** Indefinite.
**hardiness** Fully hardy.

### *Houttuynia cordata* (orange-peel plant)

A clump-forming perennial with spreading roots and erect red stems, the bluish-green, leathery, pointed leaves give off a pleasant and pungent smell when crushed. It tends to be invasive and is best containerized in a small pond. The leaves of *H. cordata* 'Chameleon' (syn. *H. cordata* 'Tricolor') are splashed with crimson, green and cream. *H. cordata* 'Flore Pleno' has pretty, green, scented leaves and double, white, green-centred flowers, but it is a thug par excellence. Unless it is contained, it will cover the ground around a large lake.

**aspect** Partial shade.
**planting depth** 5–10cm (2–4in).
**height** 45–50cm (18–20in); **spread** Indefinite.
**hardiness** Fully hardy.

*Glyceria maxima* var. *variegata*

*Houttuynia cordata*

**Juncus ensifolius (soft rush)**

Commonly referred to as rushes, the 220 species in this genus, with their flattened stems sheathed at the base, resemble many grasses. The stems are cylindrical in shape, and the leaves, when present, are small and narrow, often reduced to basal sheaths. *J. ensifolius* is a smaller variety that is ideal for the side of a small pool or a tiny natural stream. Attractive, round, brown flower-heads appear during the summer.

**aspect** Full sun.

**planting depth** 5cm (2in).

**height** 30cm (1ft); **spread** Indefinite.

**hardiness** Fully hardy.

**Lysichiton americanus (yellow skunk cabbage)**

The early spring display of yellow flower spathes has a rather unfortunate smell, hence the common name. They are followed by huge, almost stalkless, paddle-like leaves that may grow to 1.2m (4ft) high and spread to 90cm (3ft). It is slow to establish.

**aspect** Full sun.

**planting depth** Up to 2.5cm (1in).

**height** 1.2m (4ft); **spread** 90cm (3ft).

**hardiness** Fully hardy.

**Mentha aquatica (watermint)**

This common perennial has wonderfully aromatic leaves on purple stems and dense spherical clusters of tiny, lilac flowers during the summer. It is able to survive in a wide range of water depths, but does best at a depth of no more than 15cm (6in). It is best grown in large wild gardens.

**aspect** Full sun or partial shade.

**planting depth** Up to 15cm (6in).

**height** 90cm (3ft); **spread** 90cm (3ft) and more.

**hardiness** Fully hardy.

**Menyanthes trifoliata (bogbean)**

Thriving in acidic soils, this attractive perennial spreads quickly to colonize the edges of shallow ponds. It has clover-like, shiny, olive-green leaves and pretty pink buds during the spring that open into delicate, white, fringed flowers.

**aspect** Full sun.

**planting depth** 5–30cm (2–12in).

**height** 25–40cm (10–16in); **spread** Indefinite.

**hardiness** Fully hardy.

*Juncus ensifolius*

*Orontium aquaticum*

**Myosotis scorpioides (water forget-me-not)**

Commonly found all over Europe and Australia, this is one of the best marginal plants. From late spring until late summer, this delicate-looking plant is covered with clusters of pale blue flowers with yellow centres. *M. scorpioides* 'Pinkie' is a pretty pink cultivar, while 'Mermaid' is an improved cultivar that has darker blue blooms.

**aspect** Full sun or light dappled shade.

**planting depth** 0–8cm (0–3in).

**height** 23–30cm (9–12in); **spread** 30cm (1ft).

**hardiness** Fully hardy.

**Orontium aquaticum (golden club)**

The leaves of this perennial are large, blue-green, velvety and lance-shaped, with a silvery sheen on the undersides. The white-stalked, pencil-shaped flowers that emerge in early summer are tipped with yellow and resemble small golden pokers.

**aspect** Full sun.

**planting depth** 38–45cm (15–18in).

**height** 45cm (18in); **spread** 75cm (30in).

**hardiness** Fully hardy.

*Lysichiton americanus*

*Pontederia cordata*

**Pontederia cordata (pickerel weed)**

The genus *Pontederia* consists of five species of perennial which are found in the freshwater marshes and swamp ditches of North, Central and South America. These perfect marginal plants are easy to grow, with a neat habit and healthy constitution as well as distinctive foliage. The spires of blue flowers are extremely beautiful but, unfortunately, they may fail to open fully in cool, wet summers. *P. cordata*, the pickerel weed, is ideal for small ponds and can also be grown as a specimen plant in individual containers. It has erect, lance-shaped, ovate, glossy leaves, which both float and stand erect. From early summer until early autumn, it produces stunning blue flowers that are packed tightly in tubular spikes. Pickerel weed can look especially effective if it is planted in large groups. *P. cordata alba* has white flowers with pink flushed throats but it is less hardy than the species.

**aspect** Full sun to partial shade.

**planting depth** 15cm (6in).

**height** 45–60cm (18–24in); **spread** 75cm (30in).

**hardiness** Frost hardy.

*Ranunculus lingua*

*Sagittaria latifolia* 'Flore Pleno'

*Thalia dealbata*

*Zantedeschia aethiopica*

## RANUNCULUS

The genus name is derived from the Latin word *rana*, which means frog. Of the 400 species of temperate and tropical, moisture-loving plants in this genus, around 40 will grow quite happily in water.

### Ranunculus ficaria (lesser celandine)

This perennial herb is invasive and traditionally used internally and externally for the treatment of piles. There are numerous cultivars, with orange, yellow or white flowers.

**aspect** Sun to dappled shade.

**planting depth** 5cm (2in).

**height** 5–25cm (2–10in); **spread** 30cm (1ft).

**hardiness** Fully hardy.

### Ranunculus lingua (greater spearwort)

This is a vigorous perennial with yellow flowers, 2.5–5cm (1–2in) across. The rather sappy stems can easily be blown over on exposed sites.

**aspect** Full sun.

**planting depth** 15–23cm (6–9in).

**height** 1.5m (5ft); **spread** 90cm (3ft).

**hardiness** Fully hardy.

### Sagittaria latifolia (duck potato, wapato)

This perennial has variably sized, arrow-shaped, aerial leaves with whorls of three-petalled, white flowers from mid- to late summer. *S. latifolia* 'Flore Pleno' is the double form.

**aspect** Full sun.

**planting depth** 5–30cm (2–12in).

**height** 45–90cm (18–36in); **spread** 90cm (3ft).

**hardiness** Fully hardy.

### Schoenoplectus lacustris subsp. tabernaemontani 'Albescens' (white bulrush)

With its erect cylindrical stems and attractive cream banding, this perennial makes a bold display against a dark background. Insignificant, brown, spike-like flowers appear in summer. The variegated bulrush, *S. lacustris* subsp. *tabernaemontani* 'Zebrinus' has horizontal cream stripes on the stems that resemble porcupine quills.

**aspect** Full sun.

**planting depth** 8–10cm (3–4in).

**height** 1.2–1.5m (4–5ft); **spread** Indefinite.

**hardiness** Fully hardy.

### Spartina pectinata 'Aureomarginata' (prairie cord grass)

A very vigorous grass for waterlogged soil. It is an ideal specimen plant that may be used instead of bamboo. The leaves are pale green, turning bright yellow in autumn.

**aspect** Full sun.

**planting depth** 0–5cm (0–2in).

**height** 175cm (69in); **spread** Indefinite.

**hardiness** Fully hardy.

### Thalia dealbata

This is a showy evergreen plant with long, glaucous, blue leaves, which are dusted with a white powder. Branching panicles of tiny flowers appear from early to late summer.

**aspect** Full sun.

**planting depth** 30–45cm (12–18in).

**height** 1.8–3m (6–10ft); **spread** 1.8m (6ft).

**hardiness** Frost hardy.

### Typha latifolia (bulrush, cat's tail)

The extensive rhizomes of the plants in this very invasive genus, of which *T. latifolia* is a member, have needle-like tips. For this reason, they should be planted with extreme care because these tips are capable of puncturing pool liners. Bulrushes are only really suitable for large wildlife pools where the deep water will naturally inhibit their spread. With its strap-shaped leaves, which often reach up to 1.8m (6ft) in length, and deep brown flower spikes, this is another plant that is only suitable for large wildlife pools.

**aspect** Full sun.

**planting depth** 10–45cm (2–10in).

**height** 1.8m (6ft); **spread** Indefinite.

**hardiness** Fully hardy.

### Zantedeschia aethiopica (arum lily)

One of the most beautiful marginal plants, this distinctive specimen plant has elegant aroid spathes, which appear between late spring and early summer. This marginal originates from South Africa and so it will need winter protection if it is planted in a moist herbaceous border, but it is fully frost hardy if it is planted 30cm (1ft) below the surface of the water.

**aspect** Full sun or dappled shade.

**planting depth** 0–30cm (0–1ft).

**height** 60–70cm (24–28in); **spread** 23–45cm (9–18in).

**hardiness** Frost hardy.

## *focus on* iris

This is a large, widely distributed genus, containing about 300 mainly temperate, moisture-loving species, and it is one of the most important groups in the water garden. All species have a wide tolerance of degrees of moisture, but the three described here are the most suitable for growing with their roots submerged in water. Some other species are described in the section on moisture-loving plants.

*Iris laevigata* 'Colchesterensis'

*Iris laevigata* 'Snowdrift'

*Iris pseudacorus* 'Roy Davidson'

*Iris laevigata* 'Weymouth Midnight'

*Iris pseudacorus* 'Korea'

### *Iris laevigata* (Japanese iris)

This is a rhizomatous beardless *Laevigatae* iris with broad leaves, which reach 40cm (16in) in length. In early to mid-summer, and sometimes again in autumn, it produces two to four purple-blue flowers, 8–10cm (3–4in) across. The standards, or central petals, are much shorter than the falls, or outer petals, which have a narrow creamy splash. Native to Russia, China, Korea and Japan, these irises prefer an acid soil. The rhizomes should be planted at or just below the surface of the water. There are a number of wonderful varieties, including *I. laevigata* 'Colchesterensis' (double, pure white flowers, heavily mottled with deep purple, and with a blue margin to the falls); 'Mottled Beauty' (double, white flowers, mottled with purple-blue); 'Snowdrift' (large, double, pure white flowers, with tints of lilac or purple on the throats); 'Variegata' (single, mid- to lavender blue flowers and attractive grey-green and white-striped leaves); and 'Weymouth Midnight' (double, deep blue flowers with a white flash).

**aspect** Full sun or very light shade.

**planting depth** 8–10cm (3–4in).

**height** 60–90cm (2–3ft); **spread** 20–25cm (8–10in).

**hardiness** Fully hardy.

### *Iris pseudacorus* (yellow flag)

The ribbed grey-green leaves of this very vigorous rhizomatous *Laevigatae* iris reach a length of around 90cm (3ft). Native to Europe, Western Siberia and Iran, it prefers alkaline conditions and can be grown in moisture-retentive soil as well as in water. The species blooms in early summer and has yellow petals with brown or violet markings. There are a number of interesting varieties, including *I. pseudacorus* 'Beuron' (an unusual and quite rare variety with very large golden flowers); 'Ivory' (beautiful white flowers); 'Korea' (golden yellow flowers); 'Regal Surprise' (double flowers, with white and purple standards and yellow-blotched purple falls); 'Roy Davidson' (golden standards with darker yellow falls blotched and veined with red brown); and var. *bastardii* (clear sulphur-yellow flowers).

**aspect** Full sun or very light shade.

**height** 90–120cm (3–4ft); **spread** Indefinite.

**planting depth** 15–30cm (6–12in).

**hardiness** Fully hardy.

Iris pseudacorus 'Ivory'

*Iris pseudacorus* 'Regal Surprise'

*Iris pseudacorus* var. *bastardii*

### Iris setosa (dwarf aquatic iris)

The linear, mid-green leaves of this rhizomatous, beardless iris, which reach a length of 50cm (20in), are often red-tinted at the base. This is an ideal plant for creating a low carpet of upright foliage. In late spring to early summer, each stem bears two to 12 flowers, 5–8cm (2–3in) across, with purple or purple-blue falls and bristle-like and paler standards.

**aspect** Full sun to very light shade.
**planting depth** 0–10cm (0–4in).
**height** 15–90cm (6–36in); **spread** 8–15cm (3–6in).
**hardiness** Fully hardy.

### Iris versicolor (blue flag)

Native to eastern North America, the erect or slightly arched leaves of this rhizomatous, beardless *Laevigatae* iris reach 35–60cm (14–24in) in length. It produces branched stems with three to five red-purple or mauve petals where the standards are quite short and erect. The falls are white-veined with slight yellow tints. There are a number of beautiful varieties, including *I. versicolor* 'Dottie's Double' (mauve and white flowers with yellow patches and dark veining); 'Kermesina' (red-purple, almost claret-coloured, flowers); and 'Silvington' (purple with yellow markings on the falls).

**aspect** Full sun or very light shade.
**planting depth** No more than 10cm (4in) water above the roots.
**height** 20–80cm (8–32in); **spread** 8–15cm (3–6in).
**hardiness** Fully hardy.

*Iris versicolor* 'Silvington'

*Iris versicolor* 'Dottie's Double'

# moisture-loving plants

There is a wide range of plants that are ideally suited to the area beyond the actual margins of the pool where the soil becomes moist, but is not saturated. The art of planting this moist zone is to make it appear as much a part of the water garden as the waterlilies. Whereas many marginal plants may survive in this drier regime, moisture-lovers cannot cross into the saturated soil where the lack of oxygen will kill their roots. With ample moisture, however, the plants will grow quickly. For this reason, restraint is necessary in the density of the planting, as for the shallow-water plants, because they will quickly become overgrown.

*Alchemilla mollis*

*Arum italicum* subsp. *italicum* 'Marmoratum'

### *Ajuga reptans* (bugle)

This creeping perennial has dark green, spoon-shaped leaves and dark blue flowers, which are held in short spires, 15cm (6in) tall, from late spring to early summer. It makes good ground cover, but may be invasive in a small garden.

**aspect** Moderate to deep shade.

**height** 15–20cm (6–8in); **spread** Indefinite.

**hardiness** Fully hardy.

### *Alchemilla mollis* (lady's mantle)

With its perfect, green, heart-shaped, downy leaves and tiny yellow flowers held on feathery sprays in early summer, this is a superlative garden plant. It tolerates virtually any growing conditions, but thrives with plenty of moisture. It is also virtually evergreen and trouble-free.

**aspect** Full sun or dappled shade.

**height** 45cm (18in); **spread** 75cm (30in).

**hardiness** Fully hardy.

### *Arum italicum* subsp. *italicum* 'Marmoratum' – syn. *Arum italicum* 'Pictum'

This is by far the best form of the species. It has dark green, arrow-shaped leaves with cream marbling and green-white spathes in summer that are followed by stout stalks with columns of vermilion berries. These are a delicacy for slugs.

**aspect** Moderate to deep shade.

**height** 30cm (1ft); **spread** 15cm (6in).

**hardiness** Moderately hardy.

### *Astilbe* × *arendsii* hybrids

This group contains several garden hybrids in an endless range of white, pink and red colours and with different foliage characteristics. Some of the colours, particularly the luminous pinks, seem

*Astilbe* × *arendsii* 'Fanal'

just too garish for a natural-looking garden, but they do have a place in a modern setting. They are easy to grow and completely problem-free. Some good hybrids include 'Elizabeth Bloom', with pale pink flowers; 'Fanal', with crimson flowers and dark green foliage; and 'Snowdrift', with white flowers.

**aspect** Light to moderate shade.

**height** 50–120cm (20–48in); **spread** 20–90cm (8–36in).

**hardiness** Fully hardy.

### *Astrantia major* (greater masterwort)

This European perennial species is native to alpine woods and meadows and is a must-have plant for a natural garden. It is easy to grow and maintain. The late spring flowers last well into the autumn and the deeply dissected leaves, which resemble flat-leaved parsley, herald the spring with a charming freshness. The species has pinky, green-white flowers, while *A. major* 'Hadspen Blood' has very deep rich red flowers and *A. major* subsp. *involucrata* 'Shaggy' has extra-large flowers.

**aspect** Partial shade.

**height** 45–75cm (18–30in); **spread** 45cm (18in).

**hardiness** Fully hardy.

### *Bergenia cordifolia* 'Purpurea'

This perennial has rich, dark purple, rounded to heart-shaped leaves that smother the soil in shady places. The spires of magenta purple flowers appear from late winter to early spring. It will tolerate heavy clay soils.

**aspect** Light to deep shade.

**height** 60cm (2ft); **spread** 75cm (30in).

**hardiness** Fully hardy.

*Astrantia major* 'Hadspen Blood'

*Cardamine pratensis*

*Darmera peltata*

*Dierama pulcherrimum*

**Camassia leichtlinii (quamash, wild hyacinth)**
Originating from Oregon, in the United States, this bulbous perennial has linear leaves, 20–60cm (8–24in) in length. It produces racemes of star-shaped, creamy white flowers in late spring.
**aspect** Sunny position.
**height** 60–130cm (24–51in); **spread** 10cm (4in).
**hardiness** Frost hardy.

**Cardamine pratensis (cuckoo flower)**
The rosy lilac flowers of this hardy perennial appear above cress-like leaves in late spring. It self-seeds very happily in humus-rich soil and a partial or fully shaded position.
**aspect** Partial to deep shade.
**height** 30–50cm (12–20in); **spread** 30cm (1ft).
**hardiness** Fully hardy.

**CAREX**
This vast genus of 1,500 or more species of deciduous and evergreen perennials is found from temperate to arctic zones. Most are fully hardy, but those from New Zealand, which usually have brown leaves, may need winter protection.

**Carex remota (remote sedge)**
This is an attractive, but rather invasive, form with short flower spikes in early summer.
**aspect** Sun or partial shade.
**height** 30–60cm (1–2ft); **spread** indefinite.
**hardiness** Fully hardy.

**Carex sriderosticha 'Variegata' (striped broad leaf sedge)**
The common name aptly describes this more slowly spreading sedge. Its pale green leaves are striped with white and flushed with pink at the base.

**aspect** Sun or partial shade.
**height** 30cm (1ft); **spread** 40cm (16in) or more.
**hardiness** Fully hardy.

**Darmera peltata – syn. *Peltiphyllum peltatum* (umbrella plant, Indian rhubarb)**
Bright red stems topped with clusters of pink flowers appear in early spring and are followed by huge, scalloped, circular leaves.
**aspect** Sun or partial shade.
**height** 90–180cm (3–6ft); **spread** 90cm (3ft).
**hardiness** Fully hardy.

**Dierama pulcherrimum (angel's fishing rod, wandflower)**
This evergreen perennial from South Africa may need winter protection in frost-prone gardens.
**aspect** Sheltered in full sun.
**height** 90–150cm (3–5ft); **spread** 60cm (2ft).
**hardiness** Frost hardy.

**DIGITALIS**
This genus of biennials and short-lived perennials is found in Europe, northern Africa as well as western and central Asia. The name *Digitalis* is derived from the Latin word *digitus* (meaning "finger") because the individual florets on the elegant flower-heads fit neatly over the fingers.

**Digitalis ferruginea (rusty foxglove)**
This robust biennial or perennial has oblong to lance-shaped, dark green leaves arranged in rosettes. The pale yellow flowers with orange veins are produced in early summer.
**aspect** Partial shade.
**height** 1.2m (4ft); **spread** 45cm (18in).
**hardiness** Fully hardy.

*Digitalis purpurea*

**Digitalis lanata – syn. *D. lamarckii* (woolly foxglove)**
All foxgloves are highly poisonous, but *D. lanata* is grown commercially as a source of digitoxin, which is used by the pharmaceutical industry for the treatment of heart conditions. This hardy plant produces a spike of cream to fawn, veined flowers in summer followed by many-seeded capsules.
**aspect** Partial shade.
**height** 90cm (3ft); **spread** 24cm (10in).
**hardiness** Fully hardy.

**Digitalis purpurea (common foxglove)**
The flowers, in very variable shades of pink and purple, appear in early summer. *D. purpurea* f. *albiflora* cannot be relied upon to come true for a second year, but removing coloured intruders may keep the stock pure.
**aspect** Partial shade.
**height** 90–180cm (3–6ft); **spread** 60cm (2ft).
**hardiness** Fully hardy.

## FILIPENDULA

Most of the species in this genus, which is found in the Himalayas, northern Asia, Europe and North America, are suitable for naturalizing in a woodland garden or a damp meadow.

### Filipendula purpurea

The fine, large, toothed leaves of this clump-forming Japanese perennial are similar to those of astilbe. In mid- to late summer, it produces tall stems bearing rich cerise, frilly flower-heads.
**aspect** Full sun or partial shade.
**height** 1.2m (4ft); **spread** 60cm (2ft).
**hardiness** Fully hardy.

### Filipendula rubra – syn. *F.* 'Queen of the Prairies'

This spreading perennial needs plenty of room to be fully appreciated. The dark green leaves are overtopped by red stems, which grow to 1.8m (6ft) in height and bear fragrant, deep peach-pink flowers from mid- to late summer.
**aspect** Full sun or partial shade.
**height** 1.8–2.4m (6–8ft); **spread** 1.2m (4ft).
**hardiness** Fully hardy.

### Filipendula ulmaria (meadowsweet, Queen of the meadows)

In summer, creamy white, fragrant flowers decorate this clump-forming perennial. The leaves of *F. ulmaria* 'Variegata' (syn. *F. alnifolia* 'Variegata') are striped and marked with pale yellow. 'Aurea' is the golden-leaved form and needs partial shade in order to maintain the beautiful golden foliage.
**aspect** Dappled shade.
**height** 60–90cm (2–3ft); **spread** 60cm (2ft).
**hardiness** Fully hardy.

### Fritillaria meleagris (snake's head fritillary)

The nodding, bell-like, spring flowers of this fritillary, which come in various shades of purple and also white, have varying degrees of exquisite checked patterning. They are perfect for growing in damp grass or in containers, provided they are not disturbed.
**aspect** Light to moderate shade.
**height** 25–30cm (10–12in); **spread** 5–8cm (2–3in).
**hardiness** Fully hardy.

## GERANIUM

There are about 300 species of annuals, biennials and herbaceous perennials in the genus, widely distributed in all temperate regions except very damp habitats. They should not be confused with pelargoniums, whose common name is geranium.

### Geranium phaeum (dusky cranesbill)

The soft green leaves, often with purple markings, are virtually evergreen. In spring, the dusky cranesbill produces the most beautiful dark purple, almost black, flowers.
**aspect** Light to deep shade.
**height** 80cm (32in); **spread** 45cm (18in).
**hardiness** Fully hardy.

### Geranium sanguineum (bloody cranesbill)

Sparsely toothed leaves typify this plant from other geraniums. In summer, it is covered with upright, cup-shaped, deep magenta-pink flowers with darker veins and white eyes. It is completely trouble-free.
**aspect** Light to moderate shade.
**height** 20cm (8in); **spread** 30cm (1ft) or more.
**hardiness** Fully hardy.

### Geum rivale (water avens)

This is a useful plant for providing spring colour and will thrive in any soil, provided it is not allowed to dry out. It is ideal for planting around natural ponds. The pretty red buds open to delicate pinky red, strawberry-like flowers. *G. rivale* 'Leonard's Variety' has coppery cream-pink flowers, while 'Album', which is shorter at 15cm (6in), blooms with greenish white flowers.
**aspect** Full sun to light shade.
**height** 30cm (1ft); **spread** 60cm (2ft).
**hardiness** Fully hardy.

### Gunnera manicata

This is the real giant of the damp garden. Huge umbrella-shaped leaves, up to 1.8m (6ft) across, are supported by thick prickly stems. Frost-hardy gunnera need generous feeding and watering to attain their gigantic proportions. In smaller gardens incapable of accommodating plants of such a vast size, *G. tinctoria* (syn. *G. chilensis*) is a more restrained plant.
**aspect** Sun or partial shade.
**height** 2.4–3m (8–10ft); **spread** 4m (13ft).
**hardiness** Borderline hardy.

*Filipendula ulmaria*

*Fritillaria meleagris*

*Geranium phaeum*

*Gunnera manicata*

### HELLEBORUS

These currently fashionable plants have very attractive flowers that not only last for a considerable length of time, but bloom in late winter, an otherwise rather bleak time of year. Hellebores are most effective when planted in groups. They look best naturalized in a woodland garden. All parts of the plant cause extreme discomfort if ingested, and contact with the sap may irritate the skin.

### Helleborus foetidus (stinking hellebore, dungwort)

These are unfortunate common names for a plant whose bell-shaped, purple-margined, green flowers are quite pleasantly scented and appear between mid-winter and mid-spring. It is the dark green leaves that smell unpleasant when crushed. An evergreen perennial, it prefers neutral to alkaline soil.

**aspect** Full sun to dappled shade
**height** 60–80cm (24–32in); **spread** 45cm (18in)
**hardinesss** Fully hardy.

### Helleborus niger (Christmas rose)

From early winter this evergreen, alkaline-loving perennial produces stout purple stems with white, sometimes strongly pink-flushed, saucer-shaped flowers with green white centres.

**aspect** Dappled shade.
**height** 25–30cm (10–12in); **spread** 45cm (18in).
**hardinesss** Full hardy.

### Helleborus orientalis (Lenten rose)

Originating from northern Greece and Turkey, this perennial produces outward-facing, saucer-shaped, white or green-cream flowers from mid-winter. This versatile plant will tolerate most garden conditions, including heavy soil.

**aspect** Dappled shade.
**height and spread** 30–45cm (12–18in).
**hardinesss** Fully hardy.

### Helleborus × sternii

The flowers of this evergreen hellebore have creamy green petals that are suffused with pink-purple on the outside, held on attractive purple stalks that appear from mid-winter until mid-spring.

**aspect** Full sun to dappled shade.
**height** 30–35cm (12–14in); **spread** 30cm (1ft).
**hardiness** Frost hardy.

*Helleborus foetidus*

*Helleborus × sternii*

*Hosta ventricosa 'Variegata'*

*Hosta sieboldiana*

### HOSTA

Hostas have a natural affinity with water, and the leaves of this clump-forming perennial have a pleasing shape. However, hostas are regarded as caviar by slugs and snails. To protect against such pests, surround the plants with a mulch of sharp grit to prevent total devastation. Alternatively, grow hostas in a container, which may be raised on "feet" to provide further protection.

### Hosta crispula – syn. H. 'Sazanami'

This species has deeply channelled leaf stalks and heart-shaped, mid-green leaves, 20–30cm (8–12in) in length, with wavy margins and tapering tips. In early summer, it bears lavender-white flowers on single erect stems.

**aspect** Light to moderate shade.
**height** 50cm (20in); **spread** 90cm (3ft).
**hardiness** Fully hardy.

### Hosta 'Krossa Regal'

In summer, the erect stems, 1.2m (4ft) tall, bear bell-shaped, pale lilac flowers. The lance-shaped, deeply veined, glaucous, blue-green leaves are 23cm (9in) long.

**aspect** Light to moderate shade.
**height** 70cm (28in); **spread** 75cm (30in).
**hardiness** Fully hardy.

### Hosta sieboldiana

This species is distinguished by the ovate, heart-shaped to round, thick, puckering leaves, which can reach 25–50cm (10–12in) in diameter. The glaucous leaves are grey-green in colour. In early summer the stems, 90cm (3ft) in height, bear bell-shaped, lilac flowers. *H. sieboldiana* var. *elegans* has slightly shorter leaves.

**aspect** Light to moderate shade.
**height** 90cm (3ft); **spread** 1.2m (4ft).
**hardiness** Fully hardy.

### Hosta ventricosa 'Variegata'

This variety has distinctive leaves, which are irregularly margined with yellow and later turn creamy white. Leafy flower stems bear tubular, bell-shaped, deep purple flowers in midsummer.

**aspect** Partial shade.
**height** 50cm (20in); **spread** 90cm (3ft).
**hardiness** Fully hardy.

*Iris sibirica*

*Ligularia dentata*

*Lobelia cardinalis*

*Lobelia fulgens*

### IRIS

The genus of moisture-loving irises (distinct from the marginal plants discussed earlier) contains about 300 species of herbaceous perennials from a wide range of habitats in the northern hemisphere. Irises are synonymous with water gardens, and a careful selection of forms will provide a lengthy flowering season.

#### Iris ensata – syn. *I. kaempferi* (Japanese water iris)

These clematis-flowered irises from Japan range in colour from white to shades of pink, lavender, blue, violet, yellow and crimson; some are plain and others have bold and elaborate markings on the petals. The leaves are 20–60cm (8–24in) long with a prominent midrib. They can flourish in shallow water during the summer but must not be waterlogged in the winter. They are the most exotic of all the irises, with their butterfly-like flowers, which are held horizontally, providing an unequalled show of colour.

**aspect** Full sun.

**height** 90cm (3ft); **spread** 30cm (1ft).

**hardiness** Fully hardy.

#### Iris sibirica (Siberian iris)

Despite its common name, the Siberian iris comes from a wide area of Europe and Asia. In the wild, it is found in damp meadows or by lakes and streams. It prefers a moist, humus-rich soil, preferably lime-free, and, while it can tolerate drier sites, it thrives when provided with plenty of moisture in spring and summer. Both easy to grow and trouble-free, the early-summer flowers have purple standards and purple falls. They are exquisitely decorated with brown and white veining. The flowers attract butterflies and some varieties may re-flower in the autumn. *I. sibirica* 'Tropic Night' has the deepest violet-blue falls and standards.

**aspect** Full sun to very light shade.

**height** 50–120cm (20–48in); **spread** 15–30cm (6–12in).

**hardiness** Fully hardy.

### LIGULARIA

The statuesque, flower-covered stems of this waterside perennial are very showy. Ligularia are best planted in small groups or grown as a fine specimen. Originating from China and Japan, they require shelter from strong winds as well as constant moisture to prevent the leaves from wilting. Though it prefers a sunny position, it prefers some shade from a strong midday sun.

#### Ligularia dentata – syn. *L. clivorum* (golden groundsel)

The large, heart-shaped leaves appear at the base of branching stems. These hold brilliant orange daisies from mid-summer to early autumn. *L. dentata* 'Desdemona' is slightly shorter than the species and has larger purple leaves with beetroot-coloured undersides and dark stems. 'Othello' is the same height as 'Desdemona', at 90cm (3ft), but has puckered, bronze-green leaves with magenta undersides.

**aspect** Full sun.

**height** 90–150cm (3–5ft); **spread** 90cm (3ft).

**hardiness** Fully hardy.

#### Ligularia przewalskii – syn. *Senecio przewalski*

This species has very attractive, finely cut, dark green leaves and nearly black stems. These carry a spire of small, delicate, yellow, daisy-like flowers from mid- to late summer.

**aspect** Full sun.

**height** 1.5–1.8m (5–6ft); **spread** 90cm (3ft).

**hardiness** Fully hardy.

### LOBELIA

This genus of annual and short-lived perennials is found in tropical and temperate regions, especially the Americas. Some species are described as aquatics, but they actually do better in a rich moist soil with winter protection.

#### Lobelia cardinalis (cardinal flower)

In late summer, the cardinal flower bears brilliant red flowers, which resemble those of salvia, and narrow, bright green to red-bronze leaves.

**aspect** Full sun to light shade.

**height** 60–90cm (2–3ft); **spread** 30cm (1ft).

**hardiness** Fully hardy.

#### Lobelia fulgens (scarlet lobelia)

The mid-green leaves of the scarlet lobelia are sometimes flushed with dark purple, while the downy, red stems bear scarlet flowers during late summer.

**aspect** Full sun to light shade.

**height** 90cm (3ft); **spread** 30cm (1ft).

**hardiness** Frost tender.

### Lobelia × gerardii 'Vedrariensis' – syn. L. vedrariensis

Throughout the summer, this perennial produces beautiful violet-purple flowers on stems that reach 45cm (18in) in height.

**aspect** Full sun to partial shade.
**height** 75–120cm (30–48in); **spread** 30cm (1ft).
**hardiness** Fully hardy.

### Lobelia × speciosa cultivars

Although perennial, these cultivars are often grown as annuals or biennials. The leaves are mid-green to ruby red and the red, pink or mauve-blue flowers appear from summer through to autumn.

**aspect** Full sun to light shade.
**height** 1.2m (4ft); **spread** 30cm (1ft).
**hardiness** Frost hardy.

### LYSIMACHIA

The larger species in this genus are ideal plants for naturalizing in woodland gardens, while the low-growing species will provide a good ground cover in the muddy soil that surrounds the edge of natural-looking ponds and small streams. The common name for this genus, loosestrife, is said to originate from the use of the plants as a deterrent to flies around working horses during the summer, thus minimizing the strife between them.

### Lysimachia nummularia (creeping Jenny)

This creeping plant has rounded leaves and small, yellow, upturned flowers during early summer. *L. nummularia* 'Aurea' is the yellow-leaved cultivar and is preferable to the green-leaved species.

**aspect** Full sun.
**height** 5–10cm (2–4in); **spread** Indefinite.
**hardiness** Fully hardy.

### Lysimachia punctata

Tall stems of bright yellow, starry blooms, which alternate with the leaves, continue to bloom through the summer. This tolerant and trouble-free plant can be invasive but it is ideal for larger or wild gardens. 'Alexander' has golden yellow flowers and variegated leaves.

**aspect** Light to moderate shade.
**height** 90–120cm (3–4ft); **spread** 45–60cm (18–24in).
**hardiness** Fully hardy.

### Lythrum salicaria (purple loosestrife)

These are very adaptable plants that will grow virtually anywhere, whether in dry conditions or submerged in water, but they need a rich, moist soil in full sun to really flourish. Native to Britain, the tall slender spires of star-shaped, rosy purple flowers appear from mid-summer to early autumn. The cultivar 'Robert' is smaller, at 90cm (3ft), and has rosy pink flowers.

**aspect** Full sun to light shade.
**height** 1.2m (4ft); **spread** 45cm (18in).
**hardiness** Fully hardy.

### Miscanthus sinensis

This is a superlative, non-invasive grass. It is problem-free, and can tolerate most soils and conditions. The erect, slightly arching leaves are blue-green. In autumn, it produces pyramidal panicles of silky, pale grey spikelets, slightly tinted with purple or maroon, on fine stems. These often tower above the grassy leaves below. There is a good collection of cultivars with some of the finest coloured foliage, including *M. sinensis* 'Variegatus', with graceful, arching leaves strongly striped with white and 'Zebrinus', which has broad, horizontal, creamy yellow bands on the leaves.

**aspect** Full sun to light shade.
**height** 1.5–3m (5–10ft); **spread** 75–90cm (30–36in).
**hardiness** Fully hardy.

### Molinia caerulea (purple moor grass)

Originating from a habitat of wet moorlands in Europe and Asia, this delightful, non-invasive grass requires acid soil and looks best when planted in large numbers in an open space. One of the great advantages of this group of grasses is that despite their lofty heights and fragile appearance, they all remain erect throughout the summer and continue to look spectacular well into the autumn. *M. caerulea* subsp. *caerulea* 'Variegata' has cream-striped leaves, growing in a tidy tuft, with pretty, purple flower-heads, 90cm (3ft) in height, from spring to autumn. *M. caerulea* subsp. *arundinacea* 'Windspiel' has fabulous purple, open flower-heads, soaring up to 1.2m (4ft) high, which dance in the wind.

**aspect** Full sun to light shade.
**height** 1.2–1.5m (4–5ft); **spread** 40cm (16in).
**hardiness** Fully hardy.

*Lysimachia punctata* 'Alexander'

*Lythrum salicaria*

*Miscanthus sinensis* 'Zebrinus'

*Molinia caerulea* subsp. *caerulea* 'Variegata'

### Persicaria bistorta 'Superba'

This beautiful cultivar enjoys the moist soils alongside pools and streams. It produces fat pokers of densely packed flowers of soft mauve-pink in mid-summer. The flowers are held above large, dock-like leaves.

**aspect** Full sun.

**height and spread** 90cm (3ft).

**hardiness** Fully hardy.`

### PRIMULA (primrose)

One of the best-loved garden plants, the primrose is a huge genus of some 400 species of herbaceous perennial, both evergreen and deciduous, many of which originate from bogs or waterside sites throughout the northern hemisphere and the Himalayas, with a few more tender species from southern Asia.

Many species of primula are suited to the moist soil by streams and informal pools, where they provide a vivid display in late spring and early summer, particularly when massed into large groups.

### Primula beesiana

Indigenous to the moist, peaty meadows of China, this rosette-forming, semi-evergreen primula is from the Candelabra group of the species. It has cerise-pink flowers arranged in whorls in tiers on long, sturdy stems in early summer.

**aspect** Dappled shade or light sun.

**height and spread** 60cm (2ft).

**hardiness** Fully hardy.

### Primula bulleyana

This semi-evergreen Candelabra primula originates from damp, fertile hillsides in China. The pale crimson flowers fade to deep orange in summer.

**aspect** Dappled shade to light sun.

**height and spread** 60cm (2ft).

**hardiness** Fully hardy.

### Primula denticulata (drumstick primula)

This robust deciduous primula from the alpine regions in Afghanistan, Tibet and China has bell-shaped, yellow-eyed, purple flowers with spoon-shaped, mid-green leaves, which grow to 25cm (10in) in length. The leaves have white undersides.

**aspect** Light sun to dappled shade.

**height and spread** 45cm (18in).

**hardiness** Fully hardy.

### Primula japonica (Japanese primrose)

In moist, shady places in Japan, this pretty deciduous primula thrives and produces red-purple to white Candelabra-type flowers from mid-spring to early summer. The cheerful flowers of 'Postford White' are, as the name suggests, pure white, but have golden yellow centres.

**aspect** Partial shade to light sun.

**height and spread** 45cm (18in).

**hardiness** Fully hardy.

### Primula prolifera

This evergreen Candelabra primula is found growing in the wild in the moist, shady regions of India, south-west China and north Burma. In late spring through to summer, it produces stout stems with fragrant, golden yellow to occasionally pale violet flowers.

**aspect** Light shade.

**height and spread** 60cm (2ft).

**hardiness** Fully hardy.

### Primula veris (cowslip)

This rosette-forming evergreen or semi-evergreen primula produces sweetly fragrant, nodding, yellow flowers.

**aspect** Light shade.

**height and spread** 25cm (10in).

**hardiness** Fully hardy.

*Primula bulleyana*

*Primula japonica*

*Primula japonica* 'Postford White'

*Primula prolifera*

*Primula vialli*

*Rheum palmatum*

*Rodgersia pinnata*

*Persicaria bistorta* 'Superba'

*Schizostylis coccinea* 'Major'

*Trollius europaeus*

### *Primula vialli*

This is a deciduous perennial that originates from Sichuan and Yunnan in China. It produces red, hairy stems, which bear almost poker-shaped spikes.

**aspect** Light shade.

**height** 30–60cm (1–2ft); **spread** 30cm (1ft).

**hardiness** Fully hardy.

### *Rheum palmatum* (Chinese rhubarb)

Often mistaken for *Gunnera*, this species is smaller but still needs considerable space to contain its huge rootstock as well as a rich soil if the bold, architectural leaves and exotic-looking panicles, covered with tiny, creamy green to dark red, star-shaped flowers, are to make the most impact. *R. palmatum* 'Atrosanguineum' (syn. *R. palmatum* 'Atropurpureum') has crimson-purple leaves that emerge from scarlet buds and turn dark green as they develop.

**aspect** Full sun to light shade.

**height** 1.8m (6ft); **spread** 90–150cm (3–5ft).

**hardiness** Fully hardy.

### *Rodgersia pinnata*

This Chinese perennial species has crinkled, dark green, glossy leaves, 90cm (3ft) in length, which are heavily veined. It produces red-green stems, which bear panicles of flowers in yellow, white, pink or red in mid- to late summer. *R. pinnata* 'Elegans' is an excellent white cultivar. As it tends to suffer from wind and sun scorch, it best grown in partial or dappled shade.

**aspect** Light shade.

**height** 1.2m (4ft); **spread** 75cm (30in).

**hardiness** Fully hardy.

### *Schizostylis coccinea* (Kaffir lily)

Originating from the stream banks of South Africa, this vigorous rhizomatous evergreen perennial has fine, sword-like leaves and showy, gladiolus-like flowers that are produced from late summer to early winter. The true species can easily overpower a small water garden, but most of the named varieties are better behaved. These include *S. coccinea* f. *alba*, the white variety; 'Major' with deep rich red flowers;

'Mrs Hegarty' with the softest pale pink petals and the more vivid 'Sunrise' with bright salmon-pink flowers.

**aspect** Full sun to light shade.

**height** 60cm (2ft); **spread** 30cm (1ft).

**hardiness** Frost hardy.

### *Trollius europaeus* (common European globeflower)

This native European perennial is often mistaken for a marsh marigold (*Caltha palustris*), which has shiny, glossy leaves, as opposed to those of Trollius which are divided and more buttercup-like. As the name suggests, globeflowers produce globe-like, golden flowers from spring to summer. Cutting back the dead flower-heads often produces a second flush of flowers in the early autumn. *T.* × *cultorum* is a group of cultivars whose flowers vary from very pale primrose yellow to dark golden yellow.

**aspect** Full sun to light shade.

**height** 75cm (30in); **spread** 45cm (18in).

**hardiness** Fully hardy..

# ferns

Ferns excel in cool, shady places in the moist soil near water. Grown for their different forms, textures and shapes, ferns provide a wonderful waterside planting in a shady area. Indeed, there are many situations in a garden where it is more sensible to site a pool in the shade rather than in the sunniest spot. A shaded pool surrounded by ferns is the epitome of peace and calm, and can be easier to maintain than a pool in full sun.

### Asplenium scolopendrium – syn. Phyllitis scolopendrium (Hart's tongue fern)

This versatile evergreen fern has beautiful, fresh green and almost undivided fronds. It does best in moist, humus-rich soils but will also tolerate poorer soils. *A. scolopendrium* Crispum Group has mid-green fronds with strongly wavy margins.

**aspect** Light to deep shade.

**height** 60–90cm (2–3ft); **spread** 60cm (2ft).

**hardiness** Fully hardy.

### Athyrium filix-femina (lady fern)

Indigenous to Britain and very widespread in the northern hemisphere, this deciduous fern has deeply dissected, lace-like fronds and prefers to be grown in neutral to acid soil. Shelter from strong winds. *A. filix-femina* 'Frizelliae' is smaller than the species, growing to 20cm (8in) tall and with a spread of 30cm (1ft).

**aspect** Light to moderate dappled shade.

**height** 1.2m (4ft); **spread** 60–90cm (2ft).

**hardiness** Fully hardy.

### DRYOPTERIS (buckler fern)

Widely seen in the northern hemisphere growing by the sides of streams or lakes, these deciduous ferns may stay green in mild winters.

### Dryopteris affinis (golden male fern)

The fronds of this virtually evergreen fern are pale green as they unfurl in spring and mature to deep dark green. *D. affinis* 'Polydactyla Mapplebeck' has semi-erect fronds with large, fingered crests at the tips.

**aspect** Moderate to fairly deep shade.

**height and spread** 90cm (3ft).

**hardiness** Fully hardy.

### Dryopteris filix-mas (male fern)

This is a deciduous fern with robust, finely divided fronds and green midribs.

**aspect** Moderate to fairly deep shade.

**height and spread** 1.2m (4ft).

**hardiness** Fully hardy.

### Dryopteris wallichiana (Wallich's wood fern)

The yellow-green fronds mature to dark green with brown midribs and are covered with brown, almost black, scales.

**aspect** Moderate to fairly deep shade.

**height** 90cm (3ft) sometimes up to 1.5m (5ft); **spread** 75cm (30in).

**hardiness** Fully hardy.

### Onoclea sensibilis (sensitive fern)

The common name of this fern is apt because, with the first frosty weather, the bright green fronds turn brown and die back until spring.

**aspect** Light to moderate shade.

**height and spread** 60cm (2ft).

**hardiness** Fully hardy.

*Osmunda regalis*

*Onoclea sensibilis*

### Osmunda regalis (flowering fern, royal fern)

This is the largest British deciduous fern. It has huge, spore-bearing fronds that turn golden brown in the autumn. It prefers very moist, fertile, humus-rich soil, which is preferably acid. The rootstock is used as potting compost for orchids.

**aspect** Full sun to light dappled shade.

**height** 1.8m (6ft); **spread** 1.5m (5ft).

**hardiness** Fully hardy.

### Woodwardia (chain fern)

This fern is found growing on moist, shady banks near water or acid bogs. Where winters are mild, they reach their full potential, producing large, arching fronds. These are broad and lance-shaped, with finely toothed leaflets.

**aspect** Partial shade.

**height** 90–120cm (3–4ft); **spread** 1.2–2.5m (4–8ft).

**hardiness** Fully hardy.

*Athyrium filix-femina* 'Frizelliae'

*Dryopteris affinis* 'Polydactyla Mapplebeck'

# bamboos

Introduced to the West in the late 19th century, many species of bamboo make wonderful foliage plants for the waterside. Many are unsuitable for small gardens due to their large size and tendency to spread. However, smaller varieties, such as *Pleioblastus auricomis* with yellow variegated leaves and *Shibataea kumasasa* take up relatively little space.

*Pseudosasa japonica*

*Shibataea kumasasa*

### *Fargesia murieliae* – syn. *Arundinaria murieliae* (umbrella bamboo)

This species is part of a genus of clump-forming evergreen bamboos, originating from the damp woodlands of China and the north-eastern Himalayas, which thrive in fertile, moisture-retentive soil. They are vigorous bamboos, bearing linear to lance-shaped leaves with yellow or dark purple nodes.

**aspect** Full sun to partial shade.
**height** 4m (13ft); **spread** 1.5m (5ft).
**hardiness** Fully hardy.

### *Phyllostachys nigra* (black bamboo)

This species is a member of a genus of evergreen bamboo from the woodlands of eastern Asia and the Himalayas. They spread through rhizomes, but form tight compact clumps in cooler temperate zones. The arching, green, young canes of this slow-growing species turn shiny ebony black after two to three years. There are also masses of lustrous, dark green leaves.

**aspect** Full sun to partial shade.
**height** 3–5m (10–15ft); **spread** 1.8–3m (6–10ft).
**hardiness** Fully hardy.

### PLEIOBLASTUS

Indigenous to China and Japan, this evergreen species of bamboo forms thickets of erect wooden canes.

### *Pleioblastus auricomus* – syn. *Arundinaria auricoma*

This species has hollow, purple-green stems and large leaves, up to 18cm (7in) in length, which are brilliant yellow with green stripes. Protect this bamboo from cold, drying winds. It will also benefit from being cut back in early spring.

**aspect** Full sun.
**height and spread** 1.5m (5ft).
**hardiness** Fully hardy.

### *Pleioblastus pygmaeus* var. *distichus* – syn. *Arundinaria pygmaea* (pygmy bamboo)

This short bamboo, which is ideal for growing in a container, has slender canes and fresh green leaves that are held in a fan-like arrangement.

**aspect** Full sun to partial shade
**height** 60–90cm (2–3ft); **spread** 1.5m (5ft).
**hardiness** Fully hardy.

### *Pleioblastus simonii* f. *variegatus*

Originating in Japan, and previously known as *P. simonii* var. *heterophyllus*, the foliage of this tall bamboo is variegated with narrow green and white stripes, with the best variegation appearing on the younger growth.

**aspect** Sun or partial shade.
**height and spread** 4m (13ft) or more.
**Hardiness** Fully hardy.

### *Pleioblastus variegatus* – syn. *Arundinaria fortunei*

This is one of the best of the variegated bamboos. It has a dense, mound-forming habit and needs hard pruning to maintain its colour.

**aspect** Full sun to partial shade.
**height** 75cm (30in); **spread** 1.2m (4ft).
**hardiness** Fully hardy.

### *Pseudosasa japonica* (arrow bamboo)

Known as the arrow bamboo because of its very straight culms, this is one of the hardiest species of bamboo. It needs room to spread and does not thrive if it is contained. It has dark green leaves, silver-grey on the underside, with yellow midribs.

**aspect** Full sun or partial shade.
**height** 4–6m (13–20ft); **spread** Indefinite.
**hardiness** Fully hardy.

### *Shibataea kumasasa*

The narrow, dark green pointed leaves of this slow-spreading, dwarf evergreen bamboo from Japan bleach white at the tips in winter. New shoots appear very early in spring.

**aspect** Moderate to partial shade
**height** 60–150cm (2–5ft); **spread** 60cm (2ft).
**hardiness** Fully hardy.

*Phyllostachys nigra* 'Boryana'

*Pleioblastus auricomus*

# practicalities

The following pages are intended to provide some practical advice and to answer those questions that commonly arise when building a pond or other water feature, from important points on siting to how to deal with green water.

## Siting

Where a feature has an open surface of water and contains plants, it will need a location where it will receive sufficient light to enable the plants to grow and flower. This is particularly important for waterlilies, which need almost total sunshine in order to flower well. Once you are satisfied that the proposed site is sunny enough, check that there are no underground hazards, such as mains' services and drains, which will obstruct excavation. Tree roots can also pose problems when excavating a pond, as well as being a nuisance during leaf fall. For closed water features, such as cobble fountains, the need for sun is less important because this type of feature seldom contains any planting.

## Size and shape

The ultimate success of a pond may be measured by the clarity of the water. This is directly related to the size of the pond, especially its depth. If a pond is too shallow or has an insufficient volume of water, it will warm up and cool down so rapidly that green algae will thrive at the expense of plants, and, in no time at all, the pond can resemble a pea-green soup. To counter this problem, ensure that the pond is at least 45cm (18in) deep in temperate climates, and, while there is no absolute minimum on the surface area, the general rule is that the larger the pond, the fewer maintenance problems you will have.

The sides of a pond should preferably be as vertical as possible so that a given area will contain the maximum volume of water to act as a buffer to rapid temperature changes. Marginal shelves, 23cm (9in) deep and wide, are recommended around the sides because they allow a wide range of plants to be grown, which only require shallow water above the roots to grow successfully and enhance the fringes of the water.

## Pond materials

There are two basic choices regarding method of construction for a new pond: flexible liners and rigid preformed units. For very small ponds, a preformed unit is easier and quicker to install for a beginner. They are available in a range of shapes, both formal and informal, but it is

**left** Large and deep pools are far less likely to be blighted by the growth of algae, which turns the water a pea green.

**right** A preformed unit is ideal for a small, formal pond with a symmetrical shape. It is relatively easy to install and you will not have to deal with the bulky folds in tight corners that can be a problem with some of the thicker flexible liners. Preformed units are available in a range of different shapes and depths for both ponds and streams.

always better to choose a relatively simple shape rather than a design with several promontories and shallow areas. Opt for the maximum volume, and, if possible, choose a resin-bonded unit because they are much stronger and make it easier to achieve a level rim. You will need to disguise the edges of the unit. This can be done easily with paving, making a preformed unit the ideal choice for a small formal pond in a paved area.

For larger ponds, flexible liners are the best choice. They are not only cheaper for a given area than a preformed unit, but they are also more versatile and can be adapted to any design, which means that you are not limited to a specific shape. Flexible liners are available in a variety of materials and thicknesses. Some materials were once manufactured in a choice of colours, but you can usually expect to find only black available now.

Concrete has been more or less superseded by flexible liners and preformed units in pool construction, but there are situations, such as the building of raised pools for fishkeeping, where a concrete lining using walling blocks provides a strong surround. This concrete shell can be painted with resin or lined with a flexible liner to make it waterproof.

## Calculating the size of liner

When calculating the size of flexible liner, allow for the depth of the sides and for a slight overlap. First measure a rectangle that encloses the shape of the pool. After measuring the maximum length and breadth, measure the depth of the pool and add twice this measurement to each dimension. The measurements for length and width represent the bare minimum of liner required. It is prudent to add about 30cm (12in) to each measurement to provide a small overlap of 15cm (6in) on each side.

One rectangle of liner can be used for a variety of pool shapes, including designs with narrow waists to make a crossing point, for example. Where the wastage would be excessive for very narrow sections, smaller pieces of some types of liner can be welded together at specialist suppliers or taped together on site using proprietary waterproof joining tapes.

## Protecting flexible liners

As a precaution, an underlay should always be used with a flexible liner to serve as a protection against sharp surfaces. When a pool is full of water, there is considerable pressure on the bottom and sides, which can cause hairline cracks when they touch the edge of a sharp stone. Underlays, like liners, come in different thicknesses, and, on very stony ground where there are flinty pieces in the soil, choose the maximum thickness available. Soft sand can be used on the bottom of the excavation in combination with the underlay as an added precaution, but as it tends to fall off the sides of the hole as the liner is inserted, it is not the ideal protection. Ensure that you use soft sand rather than sharp (horticultural) sand, which, as the name suggests, contains sharp particles that can easily pierce a liner. Old carpet is sometimes recommended, but it rots, exposing the liner to damage.

**above** A waterfall can be brought to life with an electric submersible pump.

## Pumps and filters

If you are contemplating a moving water feature, such as a fountain or watercourse, you will need a pump. The great majority of pumps now sold are submersible models, which require no more than a connection point near the pool. With the exception of some more recently introduced solar-powered pumps, all pumps run on electricity, either on mains (utility) voltage or on reduced low voltage through a transformer.

For very small water features, low-voltage pumps may be adequate, which makes installation cheaper. A solar-powered pump can deliver enough power for a small fountain, eliminating the need for installing expensive cabling from the house.

Low-voltage pumps are restricted in their output and are suitable only for small fountains or waterfalls. They are supplied with a transformer, which should be housed under cover close to the mains power socket. Because the cable from the transformer to the pump connector does not pose a threat to life if it is accidentally severed, it can be hidden under the soil or paving. Mains voltage, on the other hand, must be protected in strong casing and buried to a depth of 60cm (2ft). Concerns about mixing water with electricity are largely overcome by fitting a residual current device at the source of power, so that in the event of accidental earthing, the power is cut off in a fraction of a second.

Submersible pumps are easy to install and also reliable to use. Always seek help from a reputable supplier when deciding on the size of pump required, but remember to arm yourself with important information such as the size and volume of the pond before approaching the supplier.

If the water feature is to include a fountain, be sure that you know which type of fountain you require and what sort of height and spread you would like. Geyser jets, for example, with their frothy heads of water, need a much stronger pump than a standard fountain rose.

If you have a pump, it is reasonably easy to introduce a filter to the pumped system. This is increasingly important when the pool is heavily stocked with fish and you wish to keep the water clear. There is a bewildering variety of biological filters available, which are often supplemented by ultraviolet clarifiers for achieving pristine water.

With any electrical fitting for the water garden, always consult a qualified electrician for both advice and fitting.

## Care and maintenance

A water garden is a dynamic feature and in managing a mix of water, plants and tiny microscopic life, imbalances may occur periodically that will affect the quality of the water. Any serious problem in the balance of life in the water normally manifests itself as green water due to the rapid build-up of green algae. Although there are numerous algaecides on the market to provide a rapid cure, the problem is likely to reoccur as soon as the chemical has worn off, so it is worth checking carefully that the fault does not lie in the design or planting of the pond.

If there is adequate leaf coverage on the surface of the pond, as well as ample submerged oxygenating plants, this will help to prevent algae from flourishing. If the pond design is too shallow and there is inadequate plant life, algae will grow.

An accumulation of rotting vegetation, which leads eventually to a thick layer of evil-smelling mulm on the pool bottom, is another common problem. A heavily planted pond where some form of hygiene

**above** Duckweed can be useful in preventing green water, but it needs constant thinning.

**above** Blanketweed can be removed by twisting a stake in the water.

**above** Use a net to remove excess growth of oxygenators and floaters.

**above** Waterlily plants need dividing when their leaves begin thrusting above the surface.

is not practised will soon need a complete clean-out in order to restore balanced conditions.

To prevent leaves from sinking to the bottom of the pond, a fine plastic net can be suspended over the water. This is particularly important during the autumn months when falling leaves can be a significant problem.

Aquatics grow very quickly in a lush pond environment and need regular cutting back and division. This applies to submerged plants, such as oxygenators and waterlilies, as well as marginal plants.

Sometimes physical damage can occur to a pond lining, particularly to thin flexible liners, leading to leaks and a drop in water level. It may be an accidental fork, the claws of a dog or even the sharp point of a heron's beak as it feasts on fish in a small urban pond. Although there are repair kits available for good-quality liners, finding the leak can be more of a problem than the actual repair. The water level is often the clue as it will stop dropping just under the point of damage, so inspect this area carefully. Once you have found the source of the leak, pump out more water

so that you can work on the repair without getting it wet. Clean and dry the area around the leak with a cloth and a little white spirit (turpentine). When dry, apply the double-sided tape supplied with the repair kit and press the patch of material on to the tape. Leave this for an hour or two so that it dries out thoroughly before raising the level of the pond again.

The meshes on submersible pumps will clog quickly if there is any blanketweed near the pump. Check the intake of your pump regularly to keep it clear.

**above** In autumn, a fine plastic net will prevent leaves from sinking into the water.

**above** Tape damaged pond linings with double-sided, adhesive waterproof tape.

**above** Clear algae and blanketweed from the strainers and inlet holes of your pump.

# suppliers

**UNITED KINGDOM**

**Allison Armour Associates**
Baldhorns Park
Rusper
West Sussex
RH12 4QU
Tel 01293 871575 or
01293 871162
Fax 01293 871111
www.allisonsgarden.com
Designer of sleek,
contemporary water
sculptures

RHS Chelsea Flower Show 2000

**Fibrex Nurseries**
Honeybourne Road
Pebworth
Warks CV37 8XP
Tel 01789 720788
Fax 01789 721162
www.fibrex.co.uk
Hardy ferns

**Kelways Ltd.**
Barrymore Farm
Lanport
Somerset TA10 9EZ
Tel 01458 250521
Fax 01458 253351
www.kelways.com
Peonies and iris

**Lilies Water Gardens**
Tarn Hows
Broad Lane
Newdigate
Surrey RH5 5AT
Tel 01306 631064
Fax 01306 631693
Design, installation, unusual
and rare plant nursery
Designer: Simon Harman/
Caribbean Cascade,
pages 70–73

**Nushimo Water Features**
120 Cypress Street
London E2 0NN
Tel 020 8981 7783
Designers: Anoushka Giltsoff
& Mona Bauwens/Water
Cubes, pages 110–113)

**Outdoor Deck Company**
Mortimer House
46 Sheen Lane
London SW14 8LP
Tel 020 8876 8464
Fax 020 8878 8687
www.outdoordeck.co.uk
Design and installation (decks,
bridges and stepping stones)

**Ben Pike**
Round Trees Garden Centre
Smallway, Congresbury
North Somerset BS19 5AA
Tel and Fax 01934 876355
Designer: Bird-bath Fountain,
pages 82–85; Copper Sphere,
pages 114–117; Iluminated
Tubes, pages 120–123

**PW Plants**
Sunnyside
Heath Road
Kennignhall
Norfolk NR16 2DS
Tel and fax 01953 888212
www.pw-plants.co.uk
Bamboos, grasses and
hardy perennials

**Tabby Riley**
15 Dumont Road
London N16 0NR
Tel 020 7241 6629
Designer: Mosaic Bowl,
pages 88–91 and Mosaic
Pond, pages 30–33

**Rowden Gardens**
Brentor
Near Tavistock
Devon PL19 0NG
Tel and fax 01822 810275

**Specialist Aggregates**
162 Cannock Road
Stafford ST17 0QJ
Tel 01785 665554
Fax 01785 665929
www.specialistaggregates.co.uk
Recycled mulches and
materials, stones and gravel

**Civil Engineering
Developments**
728 London Road
West Thurrock
Essex RM20 3LU
Tel 01708 867 237
Pebbles, gravel and boulders

**UNITED STATES**

**Gardener's Supply Company**
128 Intervale Road
Burlington, VT 05401
*Tel* (800) 863-1700
www.gardeners.com

**Garden Oaks Specialties**
1921 Route 22 West
Bound Brook, NJ08805
*Tel* (732) 356-7333
*Fax* (732) 356-7202
www.gardenoaks.com

**M&S Ponds and Supplies**
14053 Midland Road
Poway, CA 92064
*Tel* (858) 679 8729
*Fax* (858) 679 5804

**Bear Creek Lumber**
P.O. Box 669
Winthrop, WA 98862
*Tel* (800) 597-7191
*Fax* (509) 997-2040
www.bearcreeklumber.com

**High Plains Stone**
P.O. Box 100
Castle Rock, CO 80104
*Tel* (303) 791-1862
www.highplainsstone.com

**Hyannis Country Garden**
380 West Main Street
Hyannis
MA 02601
www.gardengoods.com

**The Home Depot**
www.HomeDepot.com

**Plant Delights Nursery, Inc.**
9241 Sauls Road
Raleigh, NC 27603
*Tel* (919) 772-4794
*Fax* (919) 662-0370
www.plantdel.com

**CANADA**

**Aquascape Ontario**
9295 Colborne Street Ext
Chatham, ON N7M 5J4
*Tel* (888) 547-POND
*Fax* (519) 352 1357

**Aquatics & Co**
Box 445
Pickering, ON N7M 5J4
*Tel* (905) 668 5326
*Fax* (905) 668 4518

**Burns Water Gardens**
RR2, 2419 Van Luven Road
Baltimore
ON K0K 1C0
*Tel* (905) 372 2737
*Fax* (905) 372 8625

**AUSTRALIA**

**Jardinique**
Shop 6, Reginald Street
Cremorne
NSW 2090
*Tel* (02) 9908 7000

RHS Chelsea Flower Show 2000

**The Parterre Garden**
33 Ocean Street
Woollahra
NSW 2025
*Tel* (02) 9363 5874
*Fax* (02) 9327 8466

**Whitehouse Gardens**
388 Springvale Road
Forest Hill
VIC 3131
*Tel and Fax* (03) 9877

**Ponds and Pumps**
6 Parkview Drive
Archerfield, QLD 4107
*Tel* (61) 7 3276 7666

**Waterproofing Technologies**
Level 1.210 Homer Street
Earlwood, NSW 2206
*Tel* (61) 2 9558 2161

**NEW ZEALAND**

**Diane Selby Design Ltd.**
Design, Consultation & Plants
Auckland
*Tel* (09) 416 4649

**Wilson's Aquatic Nursery**
695 Glen Murray Road, RD 2
Huntly
*Tel* (07) 826 4415

# index

Page numbers in *italics* refer to illustrations.

*Darmera peltata*

*Miscanthus sinensis* 'Kleine Fontäne'

*Typha minima*

# acknowledgements

**Author's acknowledgements**
A big thanks to Caroline Davison for making this book happen; Sarah Cuttle for her fanastic pictures; Ben, Tabby, Simon, Mona and Anoushka for their original and inventive water projects; Karen, Finn and William for their wildlife garden; Beverley and Connie for their wonderful terrace; Scarlett and Daisy for being super models; Felicity for all her expert help and, finally, I would like to thank Dennis Sullivan who made this book a real pleasure to write.

**Picture acknowledgements**
All photographs were taken by Sarah Cuttle except for the following:

KEY
t = top   b = bottom   c = centre   r= right   l = left

**Peter Anderson** 36t; 36bl and br (Marwood Hill, Devon); 37 (Peter and Isobel Robinson, Suffolk); 65 (Rosemary Rogers, Yorkshire); 67 (Harlow Carr, N. Yorkshire); 108–109 (RHS Chelsea 2001/'circ Garden'/designer: Andy Sturgeon); 131tl; 131bl and br; 132cl; 133tr and br; 134tl; 135tl and tr; 136tr; 137br; 138tl and tr; 138bl; 139tl; 142tl and bc; 143tl, tc and tr; 145bl; 146t; 146ct and cb; 148tl and tr; 148bl, bc and br; 149l; 149tc; 150bl and br; 150tr and cr; 153; 154b; 155 (all); 158b; 159b.
**Jonathan Buckley** 9 (RHS Chelsea 2000/Allison Armour-Wilson's aqualens); 21 (RHS Chelsea 2000/designer: Claire Whitehouse); 23 (RHS Chelsea 2000/designer: Arabella Lennox-Boyd, featuring William Pye's 'Vortex of Water'); 25 (RHS Chelsea 2000); 39 (RHS Chelsea 2000/designer: Arabella Lennox-Boyd); 40 (RHS Chelsea 2000/designer: Mark Walker); 68–69 (RHS Chelsea 2000); 78tr (RHS Chelsea 2000); 80 (RHS Chelsea 2000); 99 (RHS Chelsea 2000); 106t (RHS Chelsea 1999); 106b (RHS Chelsea 2000); 135bl; 136bl and br; 139br; 143br; 144tr; 147bc and b; 149tr; 149bc; 151 (all); 156 (RHS Chelsea 2000); 157 (RHS Chelsea 2000).
**Simon McBride** 144bl; 145tl.
**Jo Whitworth** 16 (The Hannah Peschar Sculpture Garden, Black and White Cottage, Ockley, Surrey/designed by Anthony Paul, Landscape Designer); 17 (Amberley Japanese Garden, Devon); 18 (RHS Chelsea 1999/designer: George Carter); 50-51 (all, Baggy House, Devon/ architects: Hudson Featherstone, London); 104 (RHS Chelsea 1999/designer: Paul Cooper).

The publishers would like to thank the following garden owners, designers and institutions for allowing their gardens to be photographed for this book:

6l (RHS Tatton Park 2000); 19t (RHS Hampton Court 2000); 24b (RHS Hampton Court 2000); 26 (Longstock Park Water Gardens, Hampshire); 27 (The Rev. and Mrs. J. Hamilton-Brown, The Old Mill, Dorset); 28–29 (Karen Lansdowne, London); 30–32 (Tabby Riley, London); 35t (RHS Hampton Court 2000); 35b (RHS Tatton Park 2000); 38 (Mr. and Mrs. John Lewis, Shute House, Dorset); 41t (RHS Tatton Park 2000); 41b (Mr. and Mrs. John Lewis, Shute House, Dorset); 43t (RHS Tatton Park 2000); 44–47 (Simon Harman, Lilies Water Gardens, Surrey); 57t and b (RHS Hampton Court 2000); 60t (Longstock Park Water Gardens, Hampshire); 60b (The Rev. and Mrs. J. Hamilton-Brown, The Old Mill, Dorset); 61 (Mr. and Mrs. John Lewis, Shute House, Dorset); 66 (RHS Tatton Park 2000); 70–73 (RHS Hampton Court 2000/designer: Simon Harman); 75 (RHS Tatton Park 2000); 79 (RHS Hampton Court 2000); 82–83 (Beverley Mills, London); 87t (RHS Hampton Court 2000); 87b (RHS Tatton Park 2000); 88–91 (Simon Harman, Lilies Water Gardens, Surrey); 100t (The Rev. and Mrs. J. Hamilton-Brown, The Old Mill, Dorset); 101tl (Mr. and Mrs. John Lewis, Shute House, Dorset); 101tr (Longstock Park Water Gardens, Hampshire); 107 (RHS Hampton Court 2000/ designers: Charlotte Asburner and Susan Reddin); 110–113 (Anna French, London); 114–117 (Beverley Mills, London); 120-123 (Beverley Mills, London); 154t (RHS Hampton Court 2000); 152 (Longstock Park Water Gardens, Hampshire); 153 (Mrs. J. Piercy, Suffolk).

The publishers would also like to thank the following picture libraries and photographers for kindly allowing their photographs to be reproduced for the purposes of this book:

6tr Charles Hawes (Chaumont International Garden Festival 2000); 8 Marcus Harpur (designer: Patrick Mann); 12 Primrose Peacock (Holt Studios International); 14 Melanie Eclaire; 19b Charles Hawes (Chaumont International Garden Festival 1999); 20 Charles Hawes (Chaumont International Garden Festival 2000); 22b Melanie Eclare; 34 Richard Bryant/Arcaid (architect: Astrid Lohss); 42 Charles Hawes (Chaumont International Garden Festival 1999); 43b Melanie Eclare; 48 Garden Picture Library (Ron Sutherland); 49 Earl Carter/Belle/ Arcaid (architect: Andrew Nolan); 56 Jerry Harpur (designer: Bradley Dynuff); 58 Clive Nichols (Evening Standard/ RHS Chelsea 1998); 59 Clive Nichols (designer: Ulf Nordjfell); 62 Melanie Eclare; 64 Helen Fickling/The Interior Archive (designers: Raymond Jungles and Debra Yates); 74 Clive Nichols (designer: Wynniatt- Husey Clarke); 74–75 Clive Nichols (designer: Fiona Barratt); 76–77 Clive Nichols (designer: Trevyn McDowell); 78bl Clive Nichols (designer: Ulf Nordjfell); 86 Michelle Garrett (designers: Mona Bauer and Anoushka Giltsoff); 96 Jerry Harpur (designer: Jean-Pierre Delettre); 97t Charles Hawes (Chaumont 2000); 97b Melanie Eclare; 98 Melanie Eclare (designers: Tindale & Batstone); 100b Melanie Eclare (designers: Tindale & Batstone); 102–103 Verne (Kees Marcelis/designer: Arhnem, Holland); 105t Garden Picture Library (Ron Sutherland); 105b Garden Picture Library (Ron Sutherland/designer: Anthony Paul); 118 Jerry Harpur (designer: Topher Delaney); 119 Andrea Jones/Garden Exposures Photo Library/RHS Chelsea 2000/designer: spidergarden.com); 130tl and bl Simon Harman; 130br NHPA (Martin Garwood); 134tr Garden Picture Library (Eric Crichton); 142bl Simon Harman; 144tl Garden Picture Library (John Glover); 145tr Simon Harman.

*Nymphaea* 'White Star'